HERTFORDSHIRE CHURCHES
and other places of worship

by

JEFFERY W WHITELAW

Oldcastle Books

1990

1990

Oldcastle Books Ltd
18 Coleswood Road
Harpenden, Herts AL5 1EQ

British Library Cataloguing in Publication Data

Whitelaw, Jeffery W. (Jeffery William)
Hertfordshire Churches
1. Hertfordshire. Churches, History
I. Title
942.58

ISBN 0 948353 85 6

9 8 7 6 5 4 3 2 1

Printed by The Guernsey Press Co. Ltd.,
Guernsey, Channel Islands.

For Katie, my grand-daughter in Australia,
in the hope that she will be able to visit some
of these churches one day.

CONTENTS

CONTENTS

LIST OF PHOTOGRAPHS

HERTFORDSHIRE CHURCHES

LIST OF PHOTOGRAPHS

FOREWORD

by

The Right Reverend the Lord Bishop of St. Albans

John Taylor

It was in 1877 that the Diocese of St. Albans was created. It was carved out of the ancient Diocese of Rochester and comprises the counties of Bedfordshire and Hertfordshire. It is, therefore, a special pleasure for me, on behalf of all Christians in Hertfordshire, to commend this book.

As with any county of England, the churches of Hertfordshire are in many ways the focus of our life and history. They represent the ongoing thread of our past, our present, and of the hope of our future. I am very mindful of this as I share, week by week, the joys and aspirations of congregation after congregation, church after church.

This book will introduce you to many of the churches and chapels of this county and how they can be best appreciated. Some of you may simply wish the sheer beauty of them to wash over you like a magnificent picture or an inspiring piece of music. Others of you may particularly enjoy their various features: like some of our fine towers and famous Hertfordshire spikes; the churches that have apses with their echoes of very early Christian worship; and, because we are on the borders of the great wool producing areas of medieval England, some of our churches from the Perpendicular period are very noteworthy, some with rood screens and splendid roofs. You may be drawn to the tombs and monuments because they can recall for us, sometimes very movingly, the lives of our ancestors, the life of the community and the social conditions of the time.

Above all, I hope all readers of this book will feel drawn to the churches as centres of worship. Places where perhaps for hundreds of years men and women have loved and served God, Sunday by Sunday, and have tried to live out their faith in their daily life and service. The writer of Psalm 22 says --

"I was glad when they said to me 'Let us go to the house of the Lord'."

My hope is that this book will inspire the reader to share in that invitation.

PREFACE

The late Dean.Inge (1860-1954) called our medieval churches "our priceless legacy of beauty scattered over the whole of our countryside", but when I was asked to write a book about the churches of Hertfordshire - medieval, modern and all denominations - I did not, at first, realise the extent of the task in such a small county.

The Abbey Church of Saint Alban, now the Cathedral, was built when there was only one faith, and the medieval churches referred to were, of course, all answerable to Rome - as was all Christendom - until the Dissolution of the Monasteries and the Reformation of circa 1539. The Established Church then became Anglican but, despite Henry VIII's original blunt declaration that he was "Head of the Church", the 1559 "Elizabethan Declaration" - although it proclaimed that England would never again accept Papal power - ensured that everything was done to spare the feelings of the Catholic party.

At this point I hasten to say that I am not intending to delve deeply into church history. This is a book about *Buildings* but these few historical comments on events occurring during the decade or so after the Reformation, together with a mention of "Dissenters" or Nonconformists and the "Catholic Emancipation Bill" of 1829, are only here to draw attention to the apparent lack of buildings in those years. Despite the Establishment and a certain amount of harassment, the Puritans (with some leaving England in "The Mayflower" for the New World) and the Roman Catholics were, on the whole, finally allowed to have their worship undisturbed but where were their buildings?

This is an interesting question but this is not the place to enquire further into where, in the county, Roman Catholics celebrated Mass or Nonconformists met over, literally, 350 years - each denomination will have its own history. As far as Hertfordshire is concerned, and in the context of this book, the oldest Roman Catholic building

...

is the Chapel of St. Edmund's College, Old Hall Green; the oldest
Baptist site is in Tilehouse Street, Hitchin - although the present
building only dates from 1844 - and the Friends Meeting House,
Railway Street, Hertford, dated 1670, is the oldest purpose-built
Meeting House of the Religious Society of Friends in the world. All
the other buildings, other than those medieval churches and those
few built in the 16th, 17th and 18th centuries, are what can be called
"modern" and I must explain that where I have used the word in the
text, the word does not necessarily mean the 20th century: its use
may refer back as far as the 19th century but basically in contrast
to "medieval".

I have made no attempt to go deeply into architectural niceties and
there are not a lot of involved architectural terms: however, any
difficulties encountered in the entries in chapters 5 and 6 may be
solved by reference to The Glossary of Terms where unusual words
may be found - although words like "font" have been omitted. It is
hoped that this book will increase the visitors' knowledge and
understanding: no two churches are alike and it is hoped that the
Glossary will give added point to this. Similarly, there is no attempt
to describe the Cathedral in complete detail but I hope that chapter
2 is helpful for a better tour - and a better understanding.

In chapter 5 "What to Look for Inside a Church" or in chapter 6
"What to See Outside Churches", each item, be it "Glass" or
"Gargoyles". has a paragraph devoted to it and in each, one or two
churches are mentioned: I must mention that usually the list of
churches containing that item is probably not exhaustive and that
the full details will be found in the Gazetteer. I must make a point
here because all along I have been writing as if it was an easy matter
to visit every church but, unfortunately, this is not always the case.
In these days of ever-increasing thefts and high-speed get-aways, it
is quite understandable that churches should be kept locked when
not in use - although, surprisingly, more were found open during my
researches than otherwise. Sadly, far too often, when a church *was*
found to be locked, there was absolutely no indication as to where
the key could be located.

A number of authors like the late Sir Nikolaus Pevsner or Arthur
Mee are quoted on a number of occasions and I make no apology for
this. Sir Nikolaus Pevsner's "Buildings of England" series, published by Penguin Books, is a marvellous collection of books without

parallel covering every county which has been my "bible" and architectural inspiration ever since the books started to be published - with the 1st edition of "Hertfordshire" being one of the earliest. Likewise, Arthur Mee's book, written before the Second World War, has been helpful - albeit a little inaccurate.

Above all, I must pay tribute to the late county historian W. Branch Johnson. His books included the virtual re-writing of the Herbert W Tompkins' "Little Guide" which was published in 1953 but one of his last was a little edited version of the "Carrington Diaries" for which I took photographs for him. Perhaps he felt that his task was all but done because, in lieu of cash, he gave me his own annotated edition of "The Royal Commission on Historical Monuments - An Inventory of the Historical Monuments in Hertfordshire" - a reward which no money could equal: without this book my task would have been well-nigh impossible.

And so to a few apologies and acknowledgements. First, the Gazetteer includes every church and religious establishment - with the aid of Directories (see Bibliography) and telephone calls etc., - but I will be glad to know of any mistakes or omissions so that the matter can be put right should there be a 2nd edition: in the meantime, please accept my apology should your particular church or chapel have been left out. Many church guides and local guides as well as many books were consulted for greater accuracy - all listed in the Bibliography - and I am grateful to the writers of all these works. To any author who may consider that I have used his words without acknowledgement - research often results in only one suitable comment on the subject involved - a humble apology is again in order.

Finally, I must offer my grateful thanks to The Right Reverend the Bishop of St. Albans, John Taylor, who has taken the trouble to write a Foreword for my book and thus encourage me to think that it has all been worth while.

Rutland. June 1990 **Jeffery W Whitelaw**

CHAPTER ONE

BEGINNINGS

It has been said that the parish churches of England are the specially important contribution to the great Western heritage of Romanesque and Gothic art. This historical eminence will never be taken away but, it cannot be denied, it is an indisputable fact that church congregations have dwindled, in most localities, to such an extent that a few places of worship have had to be closed and so become redundant.

Despite this, the landscape in Britain can still show more than 16000 parish churches,and from the steeples and towers of many the bells still summon the faithful on the Sabbath Day.

Many of these churches are quite large - in some cases the only remaining structure of a monastery swept away at the time of the Reformation - but in Hertfordshire, except for isolated examples like St.Mary's, Hitchin and St.Mary's, Hemel Hempstead, the parish churches fit neatly into place without dominance even though they were - in many cases and for many centuries - the focal point of their communities.

All, that is, of course, except for The Abbey Church of St.Alban which, although it only became the "Cathedral" to the newly formed Diocese of St.Albans as recently as 1877, is the essential lynchpin in the county, and certainly dominates the City nearly as much as the Cathedrals at Ely and Lincoln - and without the physical benefit of the level fen land which they both enjoy.

Redundant churches, small congregations and an increasingly secular society notwithstanding, new churches continue to be built and nowhere more so than in Hertfordshire. The planners, in their wisdom, decided in the 1946 New Towns Act that four of the new towns to be created to absorb London's overflowing population, should be imposed on the county - albeit that one of them, Welwyn Garden City, was merely the further expansion of Ebenezer Howard's creation after the First World War.

I have used the words "imposed on the county" but this is not the place in which to discuss the merits or otherwise of the new towns and the fact remains that, in the planning, the building of new churches was not forgotten. More detailed comment will be made about these churches later but sufficient at this stage to mention as examples - mainly because of their architectural divergence from the traditional church building - St.John's at the Hilltop, Hatfield and St.George's, Stevenage even though Pevsner calls St.George's "a depressingly ugly one".

Coupled with these two New Town churches, I must also, briefly at this point, refer to a few other places of worship elsewhere in the county - again because of their styles of architecture. These are: All Saints, Harpenden; St.George's, Norton Way North, Letchworth; St.Bartholemew's R/C Church, Vesta Avenue, St.Albans; The Friends Meeting House at Hitchin and finally, The Jamia Mosque in Watford.

But how did it all begin and, more particularly, how and where did it all begin in Hertfordshire? Braun writes " practically nothing is known of the churches in Roman Britain: the solitary example discovered in Silchester (Hampshire) suggests that it was a very diminutive copy of those in Rome.

It is clear from The Bible that it was St.Paul who brought Christianity to the Gentiles, and in some versions The Epistle of Paul to the Romans is dated 60. At the end of the Epistle is the comment "Written to the Romans from Corinthus, and sent by Phebe servant of the church at Cenchrea". In that same year - the same year in which Boudicca sacked the first Roman Verulamium - it would appear that St.Paul was apprehended and, after demanding an audience of the Emperor himself (Nero at that time), he got his way and, after surviving various adventures including shipwreck off Malta, finally arrived in Rome in 62.

There does not seem to be any evidence that St.Paul had ever visited Rome previously, but it is clear from his Epistle that there must have been a substantial body of the faithful living in the city, even though the Emperor Claudius had mistakenly expelled Christians along with Jews in 49.

Without delving too deeply into precise dates and into what is usually labelled "Ancient History", the facts surrounding St.Paul and the Christians in Rome coincide with what is known of the early Roman occupation of Britain and, indeed, the whole continent.

The Romans ruled here for 400 years - from between circa 43 and circa 410 when the Emperor Honorius told the Britons that they were now on their own with responsibility for their own defences - and in that long period the native population learned much from the Romans with many becoming Roman citizens.

Christianity became the official religion of the Roman Empire in the middle of the 4th century, and so, from all these various facts it is but a short step to concluding that, with much coming and going between Rome and the conquered lands, that Christianity had been established in Britain - or at least in Eastern Britain - quite some time before the death of the first British martyr, a retired soldier called Alban, a Roman citizen of Verulamium and a man of high social standing.

Despite these conclusions it is clear that there is nothing known about the beginnings of Christianity in Britain, and despite various legendary stories involving Joseph of Arimathea and others, no further evidence is ever likely to be found. So, with this lack of information the earliest detailed story involving Christians - at least in Eastern Britain - Christianity and a building designed and devoted solely for worship or for those who came on a pilgrimage to the shrine, must concern what some scholars refer to as the "alleged" martyrdom of St.Alban and the first modest church - probably of timber - built over the tomb on the site of the martyrdom.

There are conflicting stories about the martyrdom - legends have grown and been elaborated over the years as to where and why - but a greater controversy has been over exactly when it took place. Except in connection with the dates of actual buildings, it is not my intention to delve too deeply into history - particularly where it involves the coming of St.Augustine, St.Patrick, St.Aidan and others - but a little dissertation on the martyrdom of St.Alban is essential to the story of Hertfordshire and Hertfordshire churches.

"Alleged" or only a legend as some authorities claim, the basic story as given by The Venerable Bede in his "Ecclesiastical History" finished in 731-2 is generally accepted, although modern scholarship dates the event as happening in 209 and not 305 which was, for many years, the only date to be found in guide books. Martin Biddle, in "Cathedral and City", the book of essays published to celebrate the 900th anniversary of the foundation of the great Norman Abbey, writes "The matter of Alban is hedged about by corrupt manuscripts and massive legendary growths. Through this maze, the real facts can be reached only by a technical and scrupulously critical path".

The earliest surviving account runs more or less like this, and it starts with the stark knowledge that the Emperor Severus, whilst in Britain between 193 and 211, ordered that all Christians should be executed.   During the persecution and hunting down of those suspected of being of the Faith, Alban, a native of Verulamium to where he had retired after honourable service in the Roman Army, took pity on one Amphibalus, a priest being hunted because of the decree.

Alban hid the priest in his house, and, in the short time during which he was given sanctuary, Amphibalus baptized his protector who helped him to escape when soldiers came looking for the fugitive, by changing clothes with him. This raises the question as to who informed the authorities especially as Alban was a respected citizen with army service behind him - but, no doubt, it was impossible to keep a stranger hidden for long and probably there were many who still had no wish to see this alien religion survive.

Alban was taken into custody and when he refused to turn his back on his new faith by sacrificing to the gods, the local Roman Governor condemned him to death.   On the appointed day, Alban was beheaded, and over the centuries the event has been so embellished with stories of miracles and unusual happenings - e.g. the eyes of the executioner are said to have dropped out after he had committed the deed - that it can be easily forgotten that, although at first it was just "another" execution to the local citizens of Verulamium, a flame had been lit - never to be totally extinguished - and as a result the inhabitants gradually became converted to the faith which he refused to abandon.

But what of the first modest church built over the tomb of the Saint? Canon Feaver, in one of the Cathedral guidebooks, writes "There is no reason to doubt Gildas when he wrote that after the persecutions

British Christians were careful to build churches in honour of their martyred brethren" and that this "can be taken as evidence that there was a Church of St.Alban on the site of the martyrdom within a few years of his death".

After the Romans left, the Angles and Saxons gradually overran South-Eastern England, and a veil descends for quite a period on the fate of the Christians.   The Saxons, of course, had their own Christian community and it is on record that Germain, Bishop of Auxerre - later to be St.Germanus - visited the tomb when he came over from the Continent in 429 to attend a Synod at Verulamium which shows that there was still an active Christian presence in the city. This was only 20 or so years after the departure of the legions but, at some time in the Dark Ages which followed, the tomb became, at first, inaccessible because, after the disintegration of Roman Verulamium, incoming pagan Saxon settlers surrounded it, and then, later, marauding Danes are credited with destroying that first church about which we know little or nothing.

At this point it would seem pertinent to leave the evolution of the future Cathedral with this desecration by the Danes and the story will be taken up again in due course. Earlier I wrote that practically nothing is known about the churches in Roman Britain: regrettably, more locally, we must come to very nearly the same conclusion about the period between the departure of the Romans and the coming of the Normans - the reason being that timber would be the material of which they were made and subject to rotting away.

All, however, is not lost: stone buildings began to be built in what is known as the Later Anglo-Saxon period and, although there is nothing as large, for example, as the complete Saxon tower of St.Thomas of Canterbury Church at Clapham in Bedfordshire, T.P.Smith in "The Anglo-Saxon Churches of Hertfordshire" describes in detail the results of his researches at those churches where Anglo-Saxon remains are known to exist. These are at Little Munden, Northchurch, Reed, Walkern, Westmill, Wheathampstead and at both St.Michael's and St.Stephen's in St.Albans together with some Saxon shafts incorporated into the mainly Norman Abbey Church.

The monograph by T.P.Smith mentioned above is a somewhat technical essay - at least in the architectural sense - but as this book, from the very beginning, has been intended for the curious layman rather than the expert, I do not intend to delve too deeply into it: the relevant and important aspects of the Saxon remains, however, in these originally Anglo-Saxon churches can be stressed without too much architectural detail.   Perhaps the most interesting visual antiquity is the north doorway - now blocked up - at St.Mary's church at Reed: this is dated Late Anglo-Saxon and there is evidence of work of a similar period to be found in the nave. Noone knows the exact date for certain and it is possible that the doorway dates from what is known as the Saxo-Norman "overlap" period - a period covering before and after the Norman Conquest.

It is clear from this Saxo-Norman overlap that no definite date line can be drawn, in architectural terms, to separate the late Anglo-Saxon churches from the very early post-Conquest Norman churches. So a little more comment on those few churches mentioned above - even if the remains, by and large, probably all belong to that overlap period - will help to round off these early "Beginnings". The blocked up north doorway at Reed is, without doubt, the most visual architectural piece of this overlap period but much of the remainder is concealed by later work.   The nave and chancel walls at St.Michael's, St.Albans are matched by the south and part of the west wall at St.Mary's, Northchurch and similarly at St.Helen's, Wheathampstead, the south and west walls of the south transept: all these are probably of pre-Conquest date. At St.Mary's, Walkern the walls are probably Saxon because they are only 2ft 3in thick but the most important relic here - especially for dating purposes - is the remains of a figure of Christ on the south wall above a former Saxon south doorway, which was destroyed by a 12th century arcade. Pevsner writes -- " It is the remains of a Rood, with the head in quite high relief but the face only slightly modelled, the body (in a tunic) almost flat, with incised drapery, surrounded by a stone frame, a combination of features characteristic of the work of the Late Saxon period."

Finally at St.Stephen's, St.Albans, there is a Saxon window in the north wall of the nave and, according to the Royal Commission on Historical Monuments in Hertfordshire, the oldest fragments of Christian architecture in the county are the turned stone balusters in the transepts of St.Albans Cathedral.

CHAPTER TWO

THE CATHEDRAL AND ABBEY CHURCH
OF ST. ALBAN

In the last chapter the version of the martyrdom of St.Alban, as given by The Venerable Bede in his "Ecclesiastical History", is the one generally accepted: he wrote -- "The blessed Alban suffered near the city of Verolamium (sic) , where afterwards when the peace of Christian times returned, a church was built, of admirable workmanship and worthy of his martyrdom --". I wrote that this church was supposed to have been destroyed by marauding Danes but, according to the 13th century historian/monk Matthew Paris, it was destroyed by pagan Saxons. He goes on to say that it was not rebuilt, although the site was still held in honour as the burial-place of the martyr. There are confusing stories about another little church built on the site of the actual martyrdom and it would appear that one escaped destruction - whether by pagan Danes or pagan English (as the Anglo-Saxons were now being called) - because of its very smallness.

A new phase in the history of the evolution of the Cathedral begins towards the end of the 8th century when King Offa II, ruler of the Mercian Kingdom, developed a conscience in his old age because he had engineered the murder of Ethelbert, King of East Anglia, when he was a suitor for the hand of his daughter Elfleda. To atone for his crime many years before, he desired to found a monastery but when he could not decide where to build, it is said that an angel visited him in a dream urging him to raise the relics of St.Alban and replace them in a more worthy shrine. King Offa and Higbert, Archbishop of Lichfield set off for what was then Saxon Verulam but discovered, on arrival, that the site of the Christian church - and, presumably, the site of the tomb itself - had been forgotten. The legend continues , however, with the story that a ray of light resolved this difficulty for them by guiding them to the spot!

I mentioned that there were confusing stories concerning a little church erected on the actual site of St.Alban's martydom and researching through half-a-dozen guidebooks or histories of the Cathedral can, literally, leave one with the problem of deciding whether there was one or two ancient churches built in the years after the martyrdom: if there were two, one was at the site of the execution - the one which had escaped earlier pagan destruction - and the other, which, when King Offa came to look for it, had presumably, being of timber, rotted away and so causing the site where St.Alban had been buried to be obliterated and forgotten. Here I must repeat some of Martin Biddle's words which I quoted earlier --" The matter of Alban is hedged about by corrupt manuscripts and legendary growths----etc" and say that to the layman, not likely to be interested in the academic discussions, the basic and generally accepted historical fact is that the present Cathedral stands on the supposed site of St.Alban's martyrdom.   Pevsner writes " The development of the site from simple Roman shrine to major medieval church must have been comparable to examples known from excavation in Germany.   In England such continuity from Roman times is unique."

Biddle argues that the "miracle", whereby the relics of St.Alban were rediscovered, cannot be accepted but, whatever the case, King Offa is credited with temporarily removing the relics of the Saint - together with other relics of apostles and later martyrs - to the little church outside the walls of Verulam which had escaped destruction: here they remained until the building of the monastery. This little church was apparently preserved and then restored by Offa before setting of for Rome to see Pope Adrian I where he obtained - according to Matthew Paris - various charters and privileges for the proposed monastery (although modern historians label these as fictitious) and after his return he founded the monastery which, no doubt, helped him to expiate his crime.

The foundation of the monastery is traditionally accepted as being in the year 793 and, although the monks were initially under the Benedictine rule, it appears that this was not strictly adhered to: circa 968-970 a strict Benedictine regime was introduced and it is from this time that the foundation of the Abbey Church can probably be dated. The first Abbot was one Willigod and he was succeeded by a dozen Abbots - some good and some bad - but little is known about the building of the monastery or of what its church consisted: the eighth abbot, Abbot Ealdred, and his successor, Abbot Eadmar had great plans to rebuild this monastery church and, accordingly, dug over parts of the site of the ruined Verulamium - no doubt doing a great deal of damage in the process - to obtain materials for the intended new building. They stored up all the stone and perfect bricks that were found in the excavations but they never started the rebuilding.

The next date which concerns us is 1077 some eleven years after William of Normandy had begun to subjugate the English after the Battle of Hastings, but a few postscripts to the Saxon era are worth a mention before moving on to the building of the great Abbey Church as we know it today. The last Saxon abbot was Abbot Frederic who only took office in the year of the invasion, 1066, and, although he was for a time the focus of resistance to the advancing Normans, it was he who, when a "cease fire" was arranged at Berkhamsted Castle, composed and administered an oath - in the words of R.L.P.Jowitt - " whereby William swore on the relics of St.Alban that he would be a 'loving lord' to them, and they on their part gave their submission to him."

There is, in fact, just one other date to go back to in the Saxon era and which is worth recording here, although the details will be found later in the book. The sixth abbot, Abbot Wulsin, (or Ulsinus as he is better known today) founded in 948 the three churches of St.Michael, St.Peter and St.Stephen - all on sites dominating the entrances to the town. One final reflection on the Saxon era: the little Saxon church built on the site of the martyrdom, spared from pagan destruction because of its size and where the relics were temporarily housed by King Offa circa 793, seems at this point in time, to drop right out of history.

And so now we come to the Abbey Church of St.Alban which, after 900 years of varied fortune including the traumas of both the Reformation and the restoration of the late 19th century, remains basically the same as when the original structure comprising the nave, transepts and the central tower were completed in 1088: it is now known as The Cathedral and Abbey Church of St.Alban.

Many books and guidebooks, both architecturally erudite and of a popular nature for the casual visitor, have been written about the Cathedral but, after quoting the words of no less an authority than the once popular broadcaster the late Professor Alec Clifton-Taylor in his book about the English Cathedrals -- " To write with any authority about English cathedral architecture in the eleventh and twelfth centuries is very difficult ", I hasten to write that the reader will find here a consensus or general agreement on the basic facts surrounding the building of the present structure. The Bibliography will provide the more assiduous student with plenty of titles to choose from if detailed study in greater depth is required: no doubt many more books can be found in libraries in the county with specialised sections dealing with Hertfordshire, its history and its buildings.

Abbot Frederic, who, as we have seen, was only appointed as head of the monastery in 1066 and who administered the oath to William at Berkhamsted Castle, was never trusted by The Conqueror and, far from being a "loving lord", William believed that Frederic was behind many of the local rebellious movements which hindered his subjugation of the country. Frederic remained abbot of the Benedictine monastery until 1077 but, after being constantly under suspicion of stirring up trouble, Frederic finally fled for sanctuary to the monastery at Ely but it is recorded that he died soon after his arrival there. William, having pinpointed where the trouble was stemming from, threatened to demolish the monastery but Lanfranc, his new Archbishop of Canterbury and a close friend, persuaded the king to stay his hand so that he could have his nephew, Paul of Caen, installed as the 14th abbot.

Paul was a really strong character and, inspired by his uncle Lanfranc who was already rebuilding Canterbury Cathedral, was full of zeal for building a new Abbey complete with all that went with a medieval monastic complex - cloisters, Chapter House, laundry, refectory, buttery and bakehouse etc. etc. Paul had no respect for the shabby buildings of the monastery of his predecessors when he took office nor, it would appear, for the Saxon abbots themselves - it is on record that he called them " Rudes et idiotas " - so almost immediately he demolished all of the old monastery except for the buttery and bakehouse which he found to be in good repair.

Abbot Paul, who was fortunate to have all the building material he needed already to hand because of the stock-piling of stone and bricks from old deserted Verulamium by the monks under Abbots Ealdred and Eadmar, proceeded to rebuild the Abbey and the other monasterial buildings at such speed that, by the year 1088, all the church and many of the other buildings of brick of his original designs were completed. Admittedly there were many additions and changes later but, even allowing for the re-use of old Roman material, this was a remarkable achievement when one considers that the building of some Cathedrals took over one hundred years.

The general shape of the church itself, it would seem, was modelled on the Norman Abbey at Caen where Paul grew up under Lanfranc's tutellage, but the completion of the work in only eleven years was, obviously, to a large extent due to the use of Roman and Saxon material - and no more so than in the massive Central Tower. This was the crowning glory of Abbot Paul's church, and it is here that the use of Roman bricks and tiles is most apparent today. Paul demolished the old monastery together with the church but preserved some of the stonework, and so the only obvious Saxon bits to be used by the rebuilders are the pillars or balusters in the triforium of the south transept.

Although this new church, built through the inspiration of Abbot Paul, was started after he took office and completed - at least in its first phase - in 1088, the consecration did not take place until 1115 even though there is no record of any further work being undertaken by his immediate successor, Richard de Albini, who had followed Paul in 1097 and so was in office at the time of the consecration. Before going on to describe briefly the later additions to the Abbey, its upgrading to the status of Cathedral in 1877 and then to describing all the features to be found in the Cathedral today, there is an interesting point to consider and one which I put forward without comment.

The building - call it Abbey Church or Cathedral - described above and consecrated in 1115 - is generally labelled in most guidebooks as 'Norman' but Hugh Braun, who has been quoted once in chapter one, has other ideas. He writes thus --" The masons who built Durham, Peterborough, Ely and St.Albans - in their day the finest buildings in the world -were Anglo-Saxons with a long tradition behind them. It is exceedingly unjust as well as misleading to call the architecture they created 'Norman'. It may with accuracy be termed 'Post Conquest' -- but 'Norman' like 'Romanesque' is a term which should be dropped forthwith." So it was Abbot Paul's inspiration but the craftsmen who carried out the work were the Anglo-Saxon masons already in St.Albans.

The new monastic or Abbey Church, which was built initially in what is - despite the admonitions of Hugh Braun - usually called the Norman period, was, on completion, 426 feet long and certainly could claim to be one of the noblest and largest structures in the land. The Norman period extended roughly from the Conquest right through the 12th century but no structural alterations were made to the church until 1195 when a new Abbot, John de Cella, lengthened three bays of the nave and rebuilt (for the first time) the original Norman west front in what became known as the Early English style: he did not , however, live to see it completed because of delays in the early stages due to squandering of funds by his first 'clerk of the works '.

These extensions and alterations were not completed until circa 1235 although some of the Early English bays of the nave were finished by 1220 after Abbot William de Trumpington had taken office in 1214. He was succeeded by John de Hertford in 1235 and there is no record of any important building work being undertaken during his term of office but, towards the end of his time, plans appear to have been drawn up for the rebuilding of the east end of the Norman building - particularly because it was in a very danger- ous condition - and for the building of a Lady Chapel. This work was started some time after 1257 and was more or less finished by the end of the century: on the other hand the Lady Chapel was not completed until some time during the abbacy of Hugh de Eversden (1309-1327). The original Norman building was 426 feet long but this last work - together with the Lady Chapel - increased the dimensions to what they are today. The Abbey now measures inside 520 feet and outside 550 feet.

It might appear from the foregoing that no work was being under- taken between the long periods of major reconstruction as described but, of course, some minor repairs, changes or replacements were always necessary and sometimes, indeed, forced upon them. In 1323, during the celebration of Mass on the day of St. Paulinus with a large multitude in the church, two of the original Norman pillars on the south side of the nave fell to the ground, one after the other, through the failure of their foundations, and soon afterwards that part of the nave roof which had rested on them fell down also. Repairs were begun almost at once and the replacement, in the Decorated style, was virtually the last major change before the Dissolution in 1539 at the Reformation. Detailed comment, together with dates, on some of the internal fittings - the Shrines of St.Alban and St.Amphibalus, the almost unique Watching Loft or Chamber, the Rood Screen etc. - can wait until after a discussion of the major, albeit controversial, restoration, towards the end of the 19th century, of the whole building by Lord Grimthorpe.

In 1539 the Abbey was dissolved, the majority of the monastic buildings were taken down to be used as building materials in secular projects but the church itself was saved by the local people who bought it for £400 and it became their parish church. This was in 1553 and at about the same time the Lady Chapel was assigned for use by the Grammar School. Various repairs and restorations took place in post-Reformation times through the following three centuries but the church gradually fell into decay - or, as one guide puts it "it gently mouldered away". Sir George Gilbert Scott, by then the acknowledged expert on church and cathedral, was called in and between 1856 and 1877 was responsible for restoration and renovation in the nave, the Lady Chapel and the tower but after his death in 1878 work had to come to a halt due to lack of funds. It was at this stage that Sir Edmund Beckett - the future Lord Grimthorpe - arrived and the whole situation changed.

Many widely differing opinions have been expressed concerning the merits, or otherwise, of Lord Grimthorpe's major restoration work - some critics have used phrases like " he committed more colossal blunders ", " monumental mistakes " and " scandalous mutilation " and more, particularly about the West Front - but this book, now that an outline of history has been covered, is primarily about what there is to be found today and so no attempt will be made here to condemn or praise what was achieved in the last quarter of the 19th century. I cannot do better here than to quote from " A Guide to St.Albans Cathedral. Royal Commission on Historical Monuments. Published by H.M. Stationery Office in 1952 ."

"After Scott's death, Sir Edmund Beckett, later Lord Grimthorpe, obtained a faculty giving him complete control over the restoration. His work may be seen nearly every- where, but its main features are the west front, which he almost entirely rebuilt, the north and south ends of the transepts, the internal restoration of the lady chapel and ambulatory and the restoration, or rather the saving, of the nave. He spent nearly a quarter of a million pounds on the task and one cannot deny that there is something to show for the money. He aroused great opposition and criticism but nobody else at the time was ready to undertake the heavy financial responsibility and it is due to Grimthorpe that there is today a cathedral at St.Albans and not a heap of ruins."

There is no need to go deeply into all the discussions and political in-fighting which took place in the middle years of the 19th century concerning what diocese St.Albans should be in - at one time tied to distant Lincoln and then to Rochester - but the new diocese of St.Albans was formed in 1877 and the first Bishop of St.Albans, although he was already 70, was the former Bishop of Rochester, Thomas Legh Claughton, whose altar tomb stands in the north transept. He had no doubts about Lord Grimthorpe's work: at a luncheon held in the "Peahen Hotel" in October 1885 after a service blessing the re-opening of the restored nave, he said " Surely I am the most fortunate of bishops, for when my cathedral was tumbling down a great layman came forward to build it up again ".

And so to the major work of the late 20th century. After the dissolution, when the monastery buildings were systematically razed to the ground for use as secular building material, the great Cloister and the Chapter house were not spared either - even though they were literally part of the Abbey Church itself - and, as we have seen, the church itself was only saved from destruction because the people of the town paid £400 for it. Every Cathedral used to have a Chapter House and at St.Albans, as at many other places, it was the administrative centre for the whole monasterial complex, and next in dignity to the church. After nearly four and a half centuries, the Dean and Cathedral authorities - following a public inquiry and ex-cavations by Professor Martin Biddle on the site of the original Chapter House just south of the south transept - sanctioned a new Chapter House which was opened by Queen Elizabeth 11 on 8th July 1982.

The basic history of the Cathedral has been outlined above but the fitments in the interior - including the Shrine which makes St.Albans the unique place which it is - have been neglected and so, before continuing with the history of the growth of the parish churches (and others) in the county, a few words about the principal monu-ments will make this account of The Cathedral and Abbey Church of St.Alban more complete. There are, of course, many useful and more portable guides on sale to carry round whilst on a tour of the Cathedral, but the basic history, without the principal monuments, would not be complete. I must add one last word at this point before touring the Cathedral. A cathedral is the principal church within a diocese where the Bishop has his throne - 'cathedra' is Greek for a chair or seat - and in no way should it be considered to be a museum: it should not be forgotten that, unlike many of the large cathedrals elsewhere, that St. Albans Abbey, bought by the people of the town for £400 in 1553, is still a parish church and a place of worship.

The Shrine of St.Alban.

It was Abbot Geoffrey de Gorham (1119-1146) who placed the relics of St.Alban in a new shrine soon after the consecration of the Abbey, but Abbot Simon (1167-1183)) completed and embellished it after raising it so that it could be seen from the High Altar. After the rebuilding of the east end at the end of the 13th century, which has already been described, there emerged a finer setting for both The Shrine and for the High Altar: they were later, however, separated by the great stone screen erected by Abbot William de Wallingford (1476-1492) and dedicated in 1484. At the Dissolution the Shrine was demolished and used as part of a wall separating the Lady Chapel from the rest of the Abbey. When the wall, in its turn, was demolished as part of the 19th century restoration work and after hundreds of pieces of Purbeck marble were discovered, it was realised that the remains of The Shrine had been discovered. Although nearly three and a half centuries had passed, a fragment of Purbeck marble on the original site was the clue to the identification and now, after very clever and painstaking re-assembling of some two thousand pieces into what is thought only to be the pedestal, the remains of The Shrine stands today on the site which it occupied centuries ago.

The Watching Chamber

The Shrine of St.Alban is situated in the feretory - more popularly known as the Saint's Chapel - immediately east of the High Altar behind the stone screen, and on the north side of the Shrine pedestal is the almost unique wooden Watching Chamber or Loft of circa 1400. Here a monk was always on duty to keep watch over the

Shrine - not only because of what it contained but on account of the great treasures brought by pilgrims - and, because the Loft was fitted into arches with the back facing the north chancel aisle, the same monk could watch over the Shrine of St.Amphibalus. In the cupboard below the upper chamber, relics and treasures were kept but the most fascinating thing is the frieze around the middle between the two storeys: there is a whole gallery of quaint carvings depicting - amongst other figures - huntsmen with hounds, a shepherd playing his pipes to his sheep, a wolf with a lamb in its mouth and a milkmaid milking a cow. This example of wood decoration - nearly 600 years old - is unique and deserves more than just a passing glance.

Duke Humphrey's Tomb

Humphrey, Duke of Gloucester, one of the sons of King Henry IV and a brother of the future King Henry V - also credited as being the founder of the Bodleian Library in Oxford - expressed a wish during his lifetime to be buried in the Abbey Church and after his death in 1447, his tomb became the only royal tomb in the church. The coffin itself lies in a vault below a trap door and down a few steps close to the Martyr's Shrine, but the Chantry Chapel which was built in his honour opposite the Watching Chamber, is a fine piece of Perpendicular English Gothic architecture: triple arches set against great solid pillars, the whole surmounted with all kinds of crests, shields, niches for figures etc., and, it is particularly noted, there are several repeats on the stonework of what is supposed to be the Duke's badge of " daisies in a standing cup". This device is considered to signify the Gardens of Adonis - a classical " memento mori " which, according to a quote in Pevsner, may have been suggested by his friend Abbot John Bostock of Wheathampstead (1420-40 and 1452-1465).

The Iron Grille

Duke Humphrey's Chantry is separated from the south aisle of the Cathedral by a very rare treasure indeed - a beautiful wrought-iron grille consisting of 42 rectangular panels built up of vertical, horizontal and diagonal iron bars which looks like wood. This served as a token protection for the Shrine within the Saint's Chapel but there is some doubt concerning its date: for many years it was dated circa 1275 which would mean that it was in position before the

Gloucester Chantry was built, but some authorities suggest that it was contemporary with the Chantry.

The Shrine of Saint Amphibalus

Amphibalus, the priest who was helped to escape by St.Alban, was himself finally captured and suffered a similar fate along with some companions: they were all, so the story was handed down, buried in the Redbourn area. During the time of Abbot Simon (1167-1183) a parishioner had a "vision" in which Saint Alban himself, in a dream, led this worthy to where Amphibalus was buried. The Abbot had excavations made, some bones were, indeed discovered and - whether authentic or not - the remains of the now sanctified Saint were duly and solemnly interred in another shrine which originally stood in the retrochoir. At the Dissolution this was also destroyed but, like that of St.Alban, the bits of the shrine were used as building material and when discovered during the 19th century restorations, were also painstakingly put together again. This shrine, unlike the marble of The Shrine of St.Alban, is only of clunch and, of course, is virtually only the pedestal of the original broken up in 1539. This Shrine now stands in the north aisle opposite the back of the Watching Chamber.

The High Altar and the High Altar Screen

Abbot William of Wallingford (1476-1492) built the magnificent stone screen behind the High Altar between the Choir and the Saint's Chapel in order to make the Shrine more private - originally the monks' stalls reached right up to the High Altar - and this screen was dedicated in 1484. Fortunately it escaped complete destruction at the Dissolution although all the original statues were removed and destroyed. For more than three centuries the damaged screen was neglected until, after Lord Grimthorpe's restorations, Lord Aldenham funded a whole new series of statues, which were sculpted by Harry Hems of Exeter between 1884 and 1890. There has been a certain amount of discussion over the merits of these statues but it cannot be denied that this High Alar Screen makes a most impressive sight. The reredos above the Altar, which depicts The Resurrection entitled "Christ in Majesty", is a relief by Sir Alfred Gilbert who is probably better known for his Statue of Eros in Piccadilly Circus.   On the south side of the presbytery is the Chantry Chapel of John de Wheathampstead - who, as we have seen, had two periods in office - and on the north side the Chantry Chapel of Abbot Ramryge (1492-1524).

The Rood Screen

The Screen described above is not the only stone screen in the Cathedral but the Rood Screen built by Abbot Thomas de la Mare (1349-1396), dividing the Monastic Choir from the public part of the Abbey, is the only *stone* Rood Screen remaining in an English Cathedral. This screen also held statues which were destroyed at the Dissolution but these have never been replaced like those of Harry Hems on the High Altar Screen. At one time there was what is called a "Pulpitum" one bay to the east of the Rood Screen and immediately backing on to the Choir stalls, but this has now disappeared. It is important for the serious student to know this to avoid any possible confusion arising due to some old guidebooks naming the Rood Screen and the Pulpitum as one and the same.

The Lady Chapel

We have already seen that the Lady Chapel was not completed until the beginning of the 14th century during the abbacy of Hugh de Eversden and that, after the Dissolution, it was assigned for use by the Grammar School under a charter from the crown. For more than three centuries, from about 1550 to 1870, the Chapel had to suffer from the activities of generations of schoolboys but after the School was transferred to the Great Gateway, Lord Grimthorpe restored it to its present state.

The Central Tower

The tower was part of Abbot Paul's original building and it is on the tower that the use of Roman bricks and tiles is most apparent: despite all the restoration of the 19th century the tower stands practically as it was built in the 11th century. Abbot William de Trumpington (1214-1235) erected a lead spire during his abbacy but, at some unknown later date, a shorter spire known as "the Hertfordshire Spike" replaced it. This was removed early on in the 19th century restorations because it was considered to be dangerous for the safety of the Tower.

The Chapter House

The modern Chapter House has been briefly referred to earlier but it is worth mentioning that it is the first to be built in Europe in modern times and how appropriate that it should be built on the site of the original Chapter House which was swept away at the Dissolution.   The approach to it from the Cathedral is through a beautifully restored Norman doorway in the south transept and through the "slype" where the great ornamental wooden doors are preserved.

Wall Paintings

The principal monuments have been described but before we leave the Cathedral, there are important features - dating mainly from the early 13th century - which have not been mentioned so far but which no visitor can fail to notice even on the briefest stay: these are what Pevsner calls -- " an amount of medieval Wall Painting unique among the major churches of England."

In the north-east corner of the Saint's Chapel - just to the right of the door of the Watching Chamber - is one of several paintings of Saints to be found in different parts of the building: this is St.William of York and the painting of circa 1330 is preserved behind glass. What makes St.Albans so important, however, is the almost unique series of paintings - discovered in the 19th century behind whitewash - on the west side of the north piers of the nave. Each painting is made up of two tiers with the dominant feature in each being a portrayal of The Crucifixion whilst the lower tier depicts a scene from the life of the Blessed Virgin Mary.

CHAPTER THREE

POST-CONQUEST CHURCHES AND
MONASTERIES UP TO THE REFORMATION

A description of the Anglo-Saxon and "overlap" remains has already been given - together with something of the history of the Abbey Church before and immediately after the Norman Conquest - but what of the smaller Norman churches in the county? Mention has already been made of the three churches in St.Albans which were founded by Abbot Wulsin in 948 but these churches, although founded in the pre-conquest era, should rightly be labelled as "Norman" even though there are some Saxon remains in each. It has already been pointed out that little, if anything, is known about the monastery and its church at St.Albans which was founded as the result of King Offa seeking to do penance, but it appears to have survived the ravages of the Danes. Elsewhere in the country and particularly in Eastern England - not yet a single united kingdom - the Danes had destroyed many religious establishments all down the east coast, from Lindisfarne to East Anglia: however, after King Alfred defeated them in battle and had converted their leader - Guthrum who became King of East Anglia - the situation became more stable.

The formation of parishes had begun towards the end of the 7th century or at the beginning of the 8th century, although it was probably only after the danger of further Danish incursions had receded during the 9th century - in fact, the Christian King Canute was ruler of both a more united England and Denmark during the years 1016-1035 - that bishoprics and parishes were started to be organised in earnest. The booklet " A Hertfordshire Record " published by the Hertfordshire County Council about Hertfordshire buildings in recognition of European Architectural Heritage Year in 1975 states that " by the time of the Norman Conquest there were probably thirty or forty churches endowed in Hertfordshire and of these perhaps six have left recognisable remains."

These six churches, all with some remains dating back to the Anglo-

Saxon period, were discussed in the first chapter - and there is more detail later in the alphabetical Gazetteer - but, apart from what can be seen at St.Michael's and St.Stephen's in St.Albans, there is nothing now visible of Saxon architecture. On the other hand, there is much more of the immediate post-Conquest Norman ecclesiastical building still to be seen and, although the most important architectural work in the county during the half-century after 1066 was the building of Abbot Paul's Abbey Church, there was great activity with regard to the smaller churches as well.

Most of the simple buildings of the time have been enlarged or "restored" so many times that, in the words of The Royal Commission --"hardly a stone of them remains to witness to their existence," -- but a certain number are still recognisable and none more so than St.Leonard's Church at Bengeo, now part of the county town of Hertford. This Norman church, which was built circa 1120, is, apart from the Cathedral itself, the oldest complete building in the county with various alterations and restorations over the centuries not changing the original plan of the Norman builders. The important feature here is the apse, which is one of only three in the county - the others being at Great Amwell and Great Wymondley - and these three are probably the survivors of many others: apses were known to have been in existence at Weston and Wheathampstead and there were seven apsidal chapels before the rebuilding of the east end of the chancel in the Abbey Church towards the end of the 13th century. The apse was a Norman concept but apparently not to the liking of the inhabitants and by the end of the 12th century new churches were being built with chancels having squared ends: these three churches are, apparently, three out of only about 30 or so surviving which still retain the apse in the whole country. It is, perhaps, worth mentioning here that the apse, which was added to 17th century St.Peter's in Buntingford (see Gazetteer) has no Norman connection- it dates only from 1899!

The formation of parishes proceeded apace after the Norman Conquest and by the end of the 12th century it would seem that that the actual set-up of parishes as we know it today had already been arrived at. The history of the establishment of each individual parish will, of course, be different and this is not the place to enlarge on those histories: although this is a book basically about buildings, a few examples of how the parishes - and, as a consequence, the churches - came into being are of interest although there is little

documentary information as to the date when the first Hertfordshire churches were erected.

When Abbot Wulsin built the three churches of St.Michael, St.Peter
and St.Stephen circa 950, he probably created the parishes of the
same name in the district around the Abbey.   In due course it was
found that the church of St.Peter was inadequate for the needs of
that parish and the chapelries of Sandridge, Ridge and Northaw
were formed within it in the 12th century: by the beginning of the
14th century they had become separate parishes.   In like manner,
Flamstead parish had been formed out of the large Redbourn parish
even earlier in the 12th century, and at one time the Great Amwell
parish included the larger part of Hoddesdon.   Elstree did not
become a parish until the 15th century whilst Harpenden - for long
tied to the parish of Wheathampstead - only became an independent
parish in 1859.

There is nothing quite like St.Leonard's at Bengeo elsewhere in the
county but there are considerable early post-Conquest remains to be
found at several churches: Aspenden, St.Ippolyts, Norton, Redbourn and Tewin all contain work of the either the end of the 11th
century or the beginning of the 12th century: other early 12th
century work exists at Barley, Flamstead, Great Wymondley,
Meesden, Pirton, Stanstead Abbots (St.James) and Walkern.   Later
12th century work is to be seen at - or the present church is built up
from an original 12th century nave at - Anstey, Hitchin, Ickleford,
Knebworth (St.Mary and St.Thomas), Little Hormead, Stapleford,
Stevenage (St.Nicholas) and Weston.   Grouped, also, with these
churches are those at Hemel Hempstead, Sandridge and Sarratt
and a little information about these three quite diverse buildings
will be helpful in highlighting, as examples, all the ecclesiastical
building activity which was taking place in the 11th and 12th
centuries.

St.Leonard's Church at Sandridge, one of only three churches
dedicated to that Saint in the county, on first sighting it looks fairly
modern - "unpromising" as Pevsner puts it - but if one ignores the
restorations of 1886-7 and particularly the exterior, the interior has
a great deal of interest. Although St.Leonard's is grouped with the
churches of the 12th century, the earliest part consists of the eastern
angles of an aisleless nave of very early 12th century date, together
with a chancel arch of Roman bricks: these are probably the remains

of the church consecrated by Herbert Losinga, the Bishop of Norwich some time between 1094 and 1119. There are more Roman bricks in the chancel masonry and so, along with the evidence of the chancel arch, the Royal Commission suggests that the church could have a pre-Conquest date. The most interesting feature is the late 14th century *stone* Rood screen which was inserted below the chancel arch without damage to it. All early screens were of stone but in the late 14th and 15th centuries they were of oak and now this stone screen in Sandridge is unique in the county: you will remember that the stone Rood screen in the Abbey Church is the only one remaining in a *Cathedral*.

The Church of The Holy Cross at Sarratt is a village church, built at the same time as several others in the 12th century but, whereas most were remarkably similar in their dimensions, here the nave is very short in relation to the chancel which was lengthened in both the 13th and 14th centuries. It is also very conspicuous for the 15th century tower which has what is called a saddle-back roof because the roof ridge runs North and South across the line of the main building: it is the only tower roof of its kind in the county. Sir George Gilbert Scott undertook a good deal of restoration circa 1865 but the tower, which has Roman bricks in it, was apparently left undisturbed: it has been suggested that these may have come from the foundations of a Roman house which was unearthed in 1907 near Sarratt Bottom Farm.

Earlier it was stated that the little church at Bengeo, apart from the Cathedral, was the oldest complete building in the county: at the same time it is the only one-time village church to demonstrate the plainness and simplicity of the early Norman, or, more correctly perhaps, the Anglo-Norman builders. The dates attached to this little church vary, with one authority stating 1080 whilst another gives it as "early 12th century work", and the same difficulty is found when trying to date St.Mary's Church at Hemel Hempstead, the third of the churches being used as examples of ecclesiastical building in the 11th and 12th centuries. In contrast to the other two village churches, St.Mary's is an example of a large town church but it is more than that: whichever starting date is correct, and the argument is between "circa 1140" and "circa 1160", this large town church is well over 800 years old and basically remains much as it did when it was finished in the 12th century. The austerity of the early Norman churches - also the apse - was disappearing by the time this church was started so St.Mary's was built with a square-ended chancel and there is much "zigzag" work. It is worth noting that, although the spire is of the 13th or 14th century, (and spires are rare in the county), the tower is contemporary with the rest of the Norman building.

In the 13th century there was much new ecclesiastical building and, although there was important work being done in the Abbey Church at the end of the 12th century and at the beginning of the 13th century, there was also a great deal happening in the parishes. A number of parish churches, usually simple aisleless buildings and possibly with an apse like St.Leonard's at Bengeo, had been built in the early post-Conquest years but by the end of the 12th century styles and techniques had already started to change. Many chancels were rebuilt during the 13th century and in the rebuilding became square-ended with the majority of the apses disappearing, aisles were being added to accomodate larger congregations and to provide paths for processions, windows increased in size (initially just narrow openings) as glass became cheaper and, perhaps more importantly, nave walls were being raised in a number of churches above the aisle roofs so that windows - known as "clerestory windows" - could be put in to bring more light into the nave.

It is not my intention to list every church of this period as there are full details in the Gazetteer but a few features in individual churches covering some of these changes will be of interest before moving on to the next century. St.James' Church at Thorley was built simply, and still retains some of that simplicity: it was completed circa 1220, it has no aisles but a fine Norman zigzag arch over the south doorway. St.Mary's Church at Gilston is basically of the 13th century in two respects: there appears to have been a former aisleless church and one doorway, of early 13th century date, remains, but the church was probably entirely rebuilt and enlarged in the second half of the 13th century although the tower was re-constructed in the 16th century. One of the most remarkable survivals of this century is the wooden chancel screen at Gilston of circa 1270 which is incorporated into a modern screen.

In St.George's Church at Anstey, there are other medieval survivors - some rare misericords of the late 13th century although two of them are of the 17th century. There is a very early font of the 12th century with a curious design, and the chancel and both transepts were rebuilt towards the end of the 13th century although the earliest parts of the central tower and about two-thirds of the nave remain of an old Saxon church rebuilt some time after the Conquest. I have only taken a few churches at random to illustrate some of the fascinating features of 13th century architecture but, as these are all more or less to the east of the county, I will add one more on the west to even matters up. St.Peter's Church at Berkhamsted has no detailed record of buildings prior to circa 1200, but, early in the 13th century, the church apparently consisted of a chancel, central tower, transepts and an aisleless nave: the aisles of the nave were added in circa 1230.

As was seen earlier, it is at the Abbey Church that the finest architectural work of the 14th century can be found - particularly with the completion of the Lady Chapel in the early years of the century and then, after the collapse of part of the nave in 1323, its rebuilding in the Decorated style - but many fine parish churches were built, or completely rebuilt, during the years of this century. Again I will pick a few churches at random, albeit with some feature of interest, although fuller details will be found in the Gazetter: Anstey, Ashwell, Brent Pelham, Buckland, Kimpton and Redbourn are those dealt with at this stage.

St.George's Church at Anstey, with its misericords and 12th century font, has already been mentioned but it is a church with a very mixed building record. The earliest parts are the central tower and about two-thirds of the nave, which belonged to a church of late 12th century date, but there was much building in the late 13th century or early in the 14th, with the present chancel being built outside the original chancel together with both the north and south transepts. Later in this century the nave was increased in length and, probably at the same time, the north and south aisles were added. St.Mary's Church at Ashwell, another large church, has an East Anglian look which may reflect its nearness to Cambridgeshire but the imposing tower of circa 1360-80 is topped by a spike of definitely Hertfordshire appearance. The church itself is of the same period although building started in the first half of the century with the chancel being completed circa 1368 and the whole original building by 1381: north and south porches were added in the 15th century. In contrast to these two comparatively large churches, the isolated little church of St.Andrew at Buckland, just off the A.10 between

Buntingford and Reed, is dated between the churches of Anstey and Ashwell: it is on record in an old history book that in some chancel glass - unfortunately now destroyed - the year "1348" was given as the date of construction by " Nicholai de Bokeland ". It is not often that specific dates can be substantiated in this way which is why the reader has to accept the use of the word "circa" so often when dealing with medieval buildings and churches.   Still in the same north-eastern part of the county, St.Mary's Church at Brent Pelham is an example of a simple and dignified aisleless church of circa 1350 although the tower is dated about a century later.

St.Peter and St.Paul Church at Kimpton seems to fall into the Perpendicular period (between approximately 1350 and 1539) but the plan of the nave is of the 12th century with the north and south aisles being added circa 1200: however, the west tower and the two-stage south porch, together with the south chapel and the clerestory windows of the nave, are all of the 15th century. Again it can be seen that here is a church with a mixed building record but it must be realised that no church remains static - especially when one studies church histories spanning centuries.   A brief mention of St.Mary's Church at Redbourn will round off this century and here, once again, there is a most interesting mixture of building dates which can be applied to the various parts of this basically 14th century church which, incidentally, is very accurately documented.   Like St.Leonard's Church at Sandridge, the original church was conse-crated by Herbert Losinga, the Bishop of Norwich, some time between 1094 and 1119 when the building consisted of a small chancel, the present nave and, particularly, the massive west tower. The chancel was rebuilt on a larger scale circa 1340 and the south aisle was added circa 1350-1360: on the other hand, the south aisle chapel and the south porch were added in the 15th century between 1444 and 1455. Before the end of that century, the clerestory of the nave was added circa 1478 and the north aisle was rebuilt in 1497.

After the rebuilding in the Abbey Church of part of the nave - after it collapsed in 1323 - there was little major building work done before what we label as "Medieval" came to an end with the Dissolution in 1539 but, of course, the unique Watching Chamber and the splendid High Altar Screen are both of the 15th century.   In the parish churches, however, there was still much activity and our final examples of medieval ecclesiastical architecture come from

Broxbourne, Caldecote, Cheshunt, Kelshall and Tring.

St.Augustine's Church at Broxbourne was completely rebuilt and enlarged in the 15th century and, although there was an earlier church on the site, nothing remains to show the date of the original. The south chapel, dated 1476, was built by Robert Stowell who later built St.Margaret's Church at Westminster, but the most interesting feature here is the *north* chancel chapel with its two-storey vestry attached. Here the date "1522" is very much in evidence: the vestry, which is built on to the north chapel, is of the same date and design, and both structures have a continuous parapet ornamented with the arms of the Saye family and an inscription recording the date of its erection in the year 1522.

St.Mary Magdalene Church in the tiny hamlet of Caldecote, a few miles north of Baldock, is the complete antithesis of the rather grand looking church of that town and, of course, of its near neighbour, Ashwell: it was, in fact, officially declared redundant in 1975 although it had been out of use for some time. I will add a personal note here to the effect that when I visited the site, the church was in a sad and sorry state and was being rapidly overgrown by extremely tenacious bushes! On the other hand I will quote W.Branch Johnson's comment in his book "Hertfordshire" published in 1970 -- " Of all the churches in the county it is the one in which I, not a conventionally religious person, hear clearest the still small voice." This was, of course, written before the church became redundant and it has, or had, at least one interesting feature. A simple church, it was built entirely in the middle of the 15th century with the south porch being more ornamental than the rest: it is embattled and inside it is a canopied and crocketed stoup which is thought to be unique.

St.Mary's at Cheshunt is another well documented church of the 15th century - the church was entirely rebuilt between 1418 and 1448 by the then Rector of Cheshunt, Nicholas Dixon, and this is recorded on a brass in the chancel: here again no details of the earlier building remain. Of particular interest here is a low 15th century archway, filled with open tracery, at the east end of the north nave arcade, which originally gave a view of the altar under the former rood loft: in the opposite wall there is a similar archway but this is a modern addition. St.Faith's Church at Kelshall is another church entirely of the 15th century, although the aisles and the south porch were added to the chancel, the nave and the west tower at a later date in that century. The church was much restored in 1870 except the tower escaped attention.

By the beginning of the 16th century, there was probably a surfeit of churches in the land and so, taken with the many still very active monasteries, there was no great call for any new ones: it would appear, therefore, that the last major ecclesiastical work in the county before the Reformation was undertaken at the Church of St.Peter and St.Paul in Tring. Little remains of the 13th century church on the site except for part of the chancel and the tower was certainly begun in the 14th century: the tower was finished in the next century when a clerestory was added. And finally to the 16th century work: this was when the chancel was rebuilt together with the north aisle. This church is noted for the animals carved on the corbels between the arches of the arcades: a fox running off with a goose, a monkey with a book and animals fighting are some of the grotesques to be seen.

Almost 500 years have been covered in this chapter - from the Norman Conquest to the beginning of the Reformation in the middle of the 16th century - but no record of this period can be complete without some further reference to the important part that monasteries (and nunneries) played in the life of the community at large. The Royal Commission states --" The wave of religious enthusiasm, partly aroused by the Crusades, which swept over Europe in the 12th century, has left in most parts of England a record of its existence in the ruins of monastic buildings containing some of the finest architecture of which this country can boast. In Hertfordshire, however, few such marks of its influence exist. The great Benedictine monastery of St.Albans, with its immense possessions in the south and west of the county --- excluded all houses of Cistercian monks and other orders of regulars." Be that as it may, and with what was the Abbey Church of this great Benedictine monastery having been described in detail, history still records that there was a handful of religious communities living in monasteries or nunneries although, as the Royal Commission states, few remains exist.

At the time of the Conquest there were only about 50 monasteries in England but by the end of the century the number is reckoned to have risen to 130 and almost all of these were Benedictine: those in the county were cells founded by the Abbots of St.Albans who were all powerful. There were cells at Hertford, Markyate, Sopwell (in St.Albans now) and Redbourn: there are no remains of any of these except at Sopwell and the ruins off Cottonmill Lane are only the ruins of Sopwell House built on the site of a Benedictine Nunnery which was founded by Abbot Geoffrey in 1140, and that was apparently on the site of a hermitage for nuns previously attached to the Abbey. Unfortunately some maps, and even guide books, used to refer to the site as "Sopwell Nunnery" - perhaps some of them are still printed showing that error. Small houses of Benedictine nuns were also founded at Cheshunt, Flamstead and Great Munden near where, today, "Rowney Priory", a largely Victorian house stands on the site of the nunnery founded circa 1164.

The remains of an Augustinian Priory of the early 13th century are incorporated into a house now called "Wymondley Priory" which lies just about mid-way between Great and Little Wymondley. Another Augustinian Priory was founded at Royston in - and here we have a firm date according to the helpful church guide - 1184 and it was situated very near to the crossing of the ancient highways of Ermine Street (now A 10) and The Icknield Way. The Church of St.John the Baptist, with its nave and aisles of circa 1250, is a survivor of the Dissolution of the Monasteries and, although being looted and vandalized at the time, is, just like the Cathedral at St.Albans, the parish church of the town.

It is interesting to read in Royston's helpful guide --" The daily life of the Priory continued without break or much incident for nearly four hundred years.   It is true that the Prior of Royston had considerable judicial powers in the neighbourhood, and often in this border town between counties had great difficulty in maintaining law and order. There were also disputes with the powerful Order of Knights Templar etc., ----." Temple Dinsley, at Preston (2 miles south of Hitchin), is an 18th century house, enlarged by Lutyens in 1908 and now a school, stands on the site of a Preceptory of the Knights Templars founded in 1147: it was presumably Knights from Preston who were the cause of the trouble referred to in the Royston guide. When the Order was dissolved in 1312 the manor passed into the hands of the Knights Hospitallers: they held it until the suppression of the monasteries.In Hitchin itself, the 17th century Biggins Almshouses stand on the site of a nunnery founded in 1362 whilst The Priory - now largely rebuilt circa 1770 by

Robert Adam - incorporates fragments of the cloisters of a Carmelite Priory which was founded in 1317. Finally, an unlikely place to find monastic remains is at the District Offices in Ware: what is known as The Priory - for long a private dwelling house - is the Council Offices of the District Council and, in fact, never was a priory. The building was largely constructed out of the remains of a Franciscan Friary after the Dissolution and it never returned to secular use.

This is not the book in which to delve deeply into the 'whys' and 'wherefores' of the Dissolution of the monasteries - first by Cardinal Thomas Wolsey and then by Thomas Cromwell - but the accepted story is that, when Henry VIII wished to divorce Katherine of Aragon and marry Anne Boleyn, the Pope refused to annul the marriage and so the King replied with a Royal Proclamation ordering the destruction of prayer books, mass-books etc " wherein the Bishop of Rome is named or his presumptuous proud pomp preferred ---- and his name and memory to be never more remembered." This basic story - fuelled over recent years by the embroidered tale of Bluff King Hal and his many wives on film and television - is, of course, only what is remembered by most people of what is a much more complicated and involved matter. It is enough to write - in what is fundamentally a book of architecture - that Parliament followed up the King's Proclamation with passing "The Act of Supremacy" which declared the King to be the supreme Head of the Church of England.

The Act of Supremacy was passed in 1534 and soon afterwards Henry attacked Church property beginning with the smaller monasteries in 1536. The stated reason for this drastic action was " that monasteries were idle, corrupt and useless, and that they owed obedience to the Pope." In actual fact, the King wanted their wealth, which was great, and used it to bribe the nobility to support his policy. (Warner and Marten) Whatever the reason, the Dissolution took place throughout the land and as Lionel Butler says " Probably the most significant feature of the Dissolution was that it met with so little hostility or obstruction." Now, after four and a half centuries, we are just left with what the celebrated historian of English monasticism, Dom David Knowles, has called the "Bare ruined choirs."

1 The tower of the Cathedral, St. Albans, Herts.

2   The Cathedral and Abbey Church of Saint Alban, St. Albans

3   South side of nave, the Cathedral, St. Albans

4　The shrine of St. Alban, the Cathedral, St. Albans

5　The watching chamber or loft (at the shrine), the Cathedral, St. Albans

6 Saxon-Norman doorway, St. Mary's Church, Reed

7 Norman south doorway, St James's Church, Thorley

8 13th Century iron grille – Gloucester Chantry, the Cathedral, St. Albans

9 Medieval painting on nave pier, the Cathedral, St. Albans

10 "St. John the Baptist" painting, Widford

11 "Deposition of Christ", St. Leonard's, Bengeo

12   Piscina and Sedilia, St. Mary's, Baldock

13   Misericord in chancel stalls, St. George's Church, Anstey

14 Part of 15th century screen in St. Cecilia's, Little Hadham

15 12th Century Norman font, St. George's Church, Anstey

16 14th Century font, St. Mary's Church, Ware

17　St. Leonard's Church, Bengeo

18　Church of the Holy Cross, Sarratt

19 St. Mary's Church, Redbourn

20 St. Mary's Church, Ware

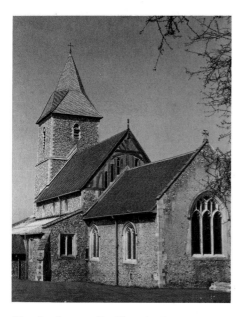

21 St. Leonard's Church, Sandridge

22 St. Helen's Church,
    Wheathampstead

23 St. Peter and St. Paul's Church, Kimpton

24 15th Century carving on benchend – now part of chair, All Saints, Willian

25 15th Century lychgate, St. Mary's Church, Ashwell

26 14th Century stone screen (view from nave), St. Leonard's, Sandridge

27 Tower of St. Mary's Church, Ashwell

28 Tower of SS. Peter and Paul Church, Tring

29 St. Mary's Church, Hitchin

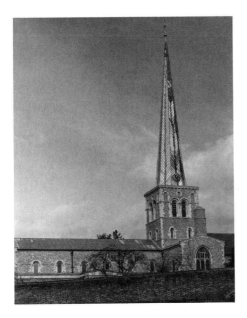

30 St. Mary's Church, Hemel
Hempstead

31 Tower of St. Mary's Church,
Standon

32 St. Ippollitts Church, Ippollitts

33 Lacon mural memorial, All Saints Church, Willian

34 Carved head in Chancel, St. Mary's Church, Westmill

35 "Wild Man" on Whittingham tomb, St. John the Baptist Church, Aldbury

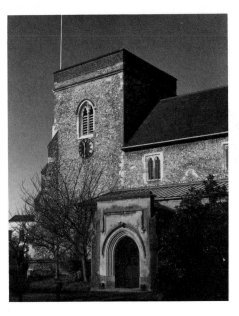

36 St. Lawrence Church, Abbots Langley

37 St. John the Baptist Church, Aldenham

38 St. Botolph's Church, Eastwick

39 St. Stephen's Church, St. Albans

40 Monument to Francis Bacon, St.
Michael's Church, St. Albans

41 Monument to Robert Cecil, 1st Earl of Salisbury, Salisbury Chapel, St.
Etheldreda's Church, Hatfield

CHAPTER FOUR

FROM THE REFORMATION
TO MODERN TIMES

A Hertfordshire Record states that ---- "With a few exceptions there was no church building in the country for the two centuries following the Reformation " and Pevsner adds the comment that " Church Architecture between the middle of the 16th century and the middle of the 17th century was stagnant." Taking these statements together, the only exception built in the county was the little Church of St.Peter at Buntingford - built originally as a chapel-of-ease to St.Bartholemew's at Layston in 1614-26: Pevsner's comment appears to refer to the fact that St.Peter's, together with the only other secular building of this period - Oxhey Chapel which was built in 1612 - were both designed in the traditional manner which had served builders well since the beginning of what is known as the Perpendicular period.

No other churches were built in the 17th century in the county - Hertfordshire had no great disaster like the Fire of London in 1666 which, in its wake, produced the great churches of Sir Christopher Wren - but it is important to remember that in the later half of the century non-conformist meeting houses began to appear: The Friends' Meeting House in Railway Street, Hertford, built in 1670, is the oldest meeting house of The Society of Friends still in use in the world. It is interesting to note that, although he lived at Shenley and is buried in the churchyard, Nicholas Hawksmoor, who seemed destined to take second place to both Wren and Vanbrugh despite his work at Castle Howard and Blenheim - not to mention the towers of Westminster Abbey- never built a church in the county. It is on record that in 1721 he published an engraving of St.Albans Abbey with an appeal for funds to --"Support this venerable pile from being Martyr'd by ye Neglect of a Slouthfull generation." I do not know whether he followed this up with any actual practical work at the Abbey: there is nothing in the text other than this appeal in Kerry Downes's biography, and the List of Works in it just has the single line which reads ----" St.Albans Abbey, Herts. Repairs, c. 1722-4."

Although there was some rebuilding in the 18th century - notably the remodelling of the chancels at All Saints, St.Paul's Walden in 1727 and at St.Mary Magdalene, Offley in 1777 - the only new church in that century was what is now known as the "New Church" at Ayot St.Lawrence built 1778-9. The "Old Church", which has a nave probably of the 12th and a chancel which was completely rebuilt in the 14th century, was still in use right up to the last quarter of the century until it became the victim of the then Lord of the Manor, Sir Lionel Lyde. In 1778 he started to build the "New" church - partly to replace the "Old" church and partly to serve as an eye-catcher from the house - in a style reminiscent of a Greek Temple. The architect was Nicholas Revett - later to design St.Pancras Church - after he had made a trip to Athens and so this was one of the first examples of the Grecian Revival in the whole country although Pevsner calls it a "purely Palladian composition." Be that as it may, the story goes that Sir Lionel arranged for the Old Church to be demolished in order to provide materials for the New but the Bishop of Lincoln (in whose diocese the parish then stood) prevented further destruction and so the Old Church building remains as a picturesque ruin - an eye-catcher itself now but, because of the possibility of falling masonry, too dangerous to visit!

The "New" Church of St.Lawrence was, indeed, the only new church built in the county in the 18th century but mention must be made of St.Andrew's Church at Totteridge - now, of course, in Greater London but for centuries, like Barnet, in Hertfordshire - which will be included in the Gazetteer. It appears only to have retained the date of when it was rebuilt and, although dates of some of the fittings from the old church are known, there does not seem to be a record of the date of the original building on the site. It was entirely rebuilt in 1790 and it has two bells from 1617 in a weather-boarded bell-turret also a pulpit of the early 17th century.

It has been demonstrated quite clearly that little in the way of church building - apart from those described - took place in virtually two and a half centuries since The Reformation but, with the coming of the 19th century, all that was to change. The population of the country had begun to grow continuously in the middle of the 18th century - largely as a consequence of a fall in the death rate and particularly in the death rate of infants - and it is clear that, as Phyllis Deane tells us in her book "The First Industrial Revolution" ----" by the end of the century the changes in the birth and death rates had been such as to constitute a demographic revolution." As I wrote earlier, this is basically a book about architecture and so I have no intention of discussing the pros and cons of The Industrial Revolution which, in the emotive and descriptive phrase "dark satanic mills", barely affected Hertfordshire.   It must be said, however, that whereas in 1770 the population was only around 7,000,000, by 1851 it was in the region of 18,000,000 with the Grand Union Canal (finished at the end of the 18th century) already being overtaken by the rapidly expanding railway system: the population of the county, like everywhere else, was growing and, the country still being basically a church-going one, there was plainly a need for new churches.

The 19th century, as far as church building in the county was concerned, began quietly and the only church built in the first quarter would appear to be that of St.Peter's in 1825 at London Colney in a style considered to be "Norman Revival".   It was during the second quarter and, indeed, right through the remainder of the century, that many new churches were built - sometimes rather hurriedly - and because of that some have blamed the Victorians for their lack of charm and "atmosphere".   They can hardly be dismissed because of this: they were, after all, built as places of worship where otherwise there would have been none at all.

It is not the building of the new churches which has brought down the wrath of later generations: it is what the Victorian "restorers" *did* to many medieval churches - first through what is known as "The Gothic Revival" and then later, because of mistaken ideas about making churches "tidy" and "respectable" - so much so that some authorities consider that more medieval work (such as wall paintings and Renaissance iron-work etc.) was destroyed by them than as a result of the Reformation!   In "Parish Churches" which was revised by Bryan Little in 1961, Cox and Ford write - after bemoaning that the provinces were soon producing a mushroom crop of Gothic towers and spires - " In this culminating phase the 13th century was generally the criterion aimed at, and irreparable damage was done to many ancient fabrics by efforts to wipe out the work of later centuries and restore the fancied characteristics of that period."   Gordon Slade, however, considers that the Victorians were, on the whole, fairly kind to Hertfordshire: argument still goes on, of course, from time to time about Lord Grimthorpe's restoration of the Cathedral because - as Gordon Slade writes - "After all, there is nothing like it anywhere else."

William Butterfield, Augustus Pugin, Gilbert Scott, together with other well-known architects of the 19th century, all had a hand in designing some of the new churches as well as being involved in some of the disastrous "restorations" and their work will be discussed more fully in due course: first, however, a mention of some of the new churches built after St.Peter's Church at London Colney. St.Paul's, Chipperfield heads the list in 1837, then Holy Trinity at Wareside (1841) and St.Thomas at West Hyde (1844) both designed by T.Smith: St.Mark's at Colney Heath (1845): all these churches were designed in the Norman style but a completely different looking building made a new landmark in St.Albans in 1850. No longer a church, Christ Church earns a place here - not only because of its past history but because of its striking Italianate appearance. St.Mary's at Thundridge (1853) was built to replace the old parish church of which only the tower remains: in the same year St.Nicholas at Elstree was virtually a new church although some of the material from an older church was re-used and the structure stands on the original foundations of the 15th century.

Augustus Pugin, who is often wrongly credited with being the architect of the new Houses of Parliament designed after the catastrophic fire of 1834 - Sir Charles Barry was the actual architect who commissioned Pugin to do not only most of the close Perpendicular but also nearly all of the internal detail - was a convert to Catholicism in the same year of the fire and, at the same time, had a fervent passion for a Catholic architecture: it can be seen, therefore, that he was one of the instigators of the "Gothic Revival". He built no churches in the county but he was chosen to be the architect to design the chapel for St. Edmund's, The Roman Catholic College at Old Hall Green between Ware and Puckeridge: it was to be " a chapel worthy of the traditions and ambitions of the college." The chapel was started in 1845 and it was completed by 1853 but, sadly, Pugin became insane by 1851 and had died in 1852 at the early age of forty.

William Butterfield, another Gothic-Revivalist who is probably best known for his Keble College, Oxford and buildings for Rugby School, did, unlike Pugin, build at least one church in the county - Holy Saviour's at Hitchin in 1863-5 - and was very involved in drastic restoration at Anstey, Barley, Barnet and Berkhamsted during the years 1869 and 1875.   St.Margaret's at Barley is, more or less, considered to be a "Butterfield" church even though he used much of the old material and he made his mark on the exterior: instead of a Hertfordshire spike, there is his own "Butterfield Spike" - unique to Barley.   At Barnet, he was commissioned to enlarge the original medieval St.John the Baptist Church and during the four years 1871 and 1875, he successfully remodelled and enlarged it: it is now a most impressive sight as it comes into view at the top of Barnet Hill.

On the St.Albans Road, leading out of Barnet, is Christ Church which was built in 1845 by the other named architect above, Sir George Gilbert Scott.   Scott's best-known works are The Albert Memorial in Kensington Gardens and what is known as St.Pancras Station, although, more correctly, the Midland Hotel at St.Pancras: these architectural monuments in the Gothic style, however, were only highlights in a 44-year career in which he was involved in the restoration of nearly 500 churches and 39 cathedrals or minsters. Scott was a great advocate of the Gothic style but this is not too apparent in Hertfordshire where he was the architect for six churches as well as for restoration work in a number of other churches throughout the county.   His first involvement with church architecture, after designing some workhouses and lunatic asylums, was in 1838 when his uncle, the vicar of Latimer in Buckinghamshire, commissioned him to design a new church at Flaunden to replace the ruined 13th century St. Mary Magdalene which stood practically on the Herts-Bucks border.

A few stones of the old church still lie in the undergrowth in a spinney (and not worth visiting) but the new St.Mary Magdalene was completed in 1838 in Flaunden - always with the cachet that it was "Scott's first church." In his memoirs he wrote about " the poor barn designed for my Uncle " but later he was to write " I cannot say anything in its favour - excepting that it was better than many then erected." Scott had not yet got into his Gothic stride when, in 1842, he designed Holy Trinity Church at Frogmore on Watling Street near Park Street: this is still in the Norman style and has a neo-Norman interior.   Soon after this he began his career as a restorer but, as well as Christ Church at Barnet, he was to design three more churches with the last one being dated 1867.

These churches are All Saints, Leavesden (Garston 1853), St.John's,

Bourne End (1854) and, finally in 1867, the little Church of St.Mary at Childwick Green - the estate village to Childwickbury between Harpenden and St.Albans. Scott's work of restoration in the county was undertaken at St.Katherine's, Ickleford (1859), St.Mary's, Hitchin (1859-65), St.Mary the Great, Sawbridgeworth (1866-7), St.James's, Bushey (1870-1), Holy Cross Church at Sarratt (1865-6) and others. He was also responsible for work at St.Stephen's and St.Michael's in St.Albans and, of course, was very much involved in the restoration of the Cathedral right up to his death in 1878.

There were many other architects - not quite so well known by name as the three above - but their creations were just as important to the growing congregations of the county during the second half of the 19th century. One of these was H.Woodyer who was responsible for St.Paul's, Hunton Bridge, near Watford (1865), St.Mary's, Bayford (1870-1) and St.Michael's, Waterford which is celebrated for its stained glass by William Morris, Burne-Jones et al (1871-2): another was Sir Arthur Blomfield who, after designing Holy Trinity Church in what is now the older part of Stevenage in 1861, put up no more new churches in the county but was much involved in restoration during the next 30 or so years: he is probably best remembered, however, for his chapel built in 1876 at Haileybury College, Hertford Heath. His restorations include work at St.John the Baptist, Aldenham (1882), St.Mary's, Aspenden (1873), St.Michael's, Bishops Stortford (1885), All Saints, Datchworth (1869-70), St.Botolph's, Eastwick (1872), St.Nicholas, Great Hormead (1872-3) and St.Mary's at Rickmansworth in 1890.

There is one other to add to this list of named architects - although the many who have been omitted would possibly be glad of it - and that is the name of G.E. Pritchett of Bishops Stortford: Pevsner writes of St.James's Church at High Wych that it " deserves to be specially mentioned as an eminently typical example of High Victorian design at its most revolting!" He goes on to say that this church, designed by Pritchett, is a " perversely ugly church " -- but ---- " as original in its handling of Gothic forms as anything in the Art Nouveau of forty years later": St.James was built in AD 1861 and Pevsner, fortunately, has no such dramatic comment to make about Pritchett's other churches at Therfield (1878) and Perry Green, Much Hadham.

An architect who was to design much larger churches elsewhere and later, the original London Police H.Q. at Scotland Yard - Norman Shaw - was the designer of only one in the county and that was St.John's at Boxmoor in 1873-4. Another architect, who was to earn greater acclaim elsewhere, was John Francis Bentley who, after being converted to Catholicism in 1861, set up on his own in 1862. Between 1883 and 1890 he built the Holy Rood Roman Catholic Church in Watford about which Pevsner writes: --" One of the noblest examples of the refined, knowledgeable, and sensitive Gothic Revival of that time." It was, no doubt, his success with the design of the Holy Rood church that prompted the Roman Catholic authorities in 1894, to commission him to design Westminster Cathedral in London. This was his magnum opus but the "History of Watford" claims that Holy Rood is "Bentley's Gem " and also that " a cathedral in miniature is the best description of the interior " because he was also responsible for many of the fittings. He died in 1902, but he left one more design : a chapel for St.Elizabeth's School and Home (Daughters of the Cross) in Much Hadham was completed in 1903 after his death.

A dozen or so more churches were built in the second half of the 19th century, other than those already mentioned when discussing their architects - and they will be found in the Gazetteer - but before moving on to the 20th century it is interesting to have a look at the curious situation in Hertford, the County Town, where there is a medieval castle, or, at least, the 15th century Gatehouse of it, but no medieval church. (Bengeo is now part of the borough of Hertford but for centuries it was a separate community so the little Norman Church of St.Leonard's can be left out of the discussion). St.Andrew's Church in St.Andrew's Street was built in 1869 on the site of a former church and from which the north doorway of circa 1480 remains. All Saints, now on the south side of the relief road, is another church which was rebuilt on the site of a former church: this time it was after a disastrous fire in 1891. Completed finally in 1905, the contract was secured by a firm of architects in Lancaster and, according to Pevsner, is " of good conscientious design and impressive size " but he goes on to say " The penalty of going to a Northerner for the design is that the church, built of red Runcorn stone, is completely alien in Herts."

It can be seen, therefore, that the oldest place of worship in the central part of Hertford is The Friends' Meeting House of 1670 which was restored in 1953, and which is, as has already been recorded earlier, the oldest Meeting House still in use in the world. The Roman Catholic Church in St.John Street stands on the site of a priory where the priory church was demolished a century after the Dissolution in 1539. Because the County Town is helping to close the 19th century in this chapter - there is one antiquity which, although from a much earlier century, is relevant to the discussion here: a drinking fountain at Old Cross, just off St.Andrew's Street, which was "Erected by Subscription", was constructed from fragments of the demolished Church of St.Mary The Less - with the central motif being a 13th century lancet window.

And so to the present century in which a number of unusual designs for churches have appeared and, as " A Hertfordshire Record " says --"Like it or not, we have at last left the older forms behind." In fact, however, this is something of an overstatement - although certainly it can be said of many of the new churches which were designed after the ending of the Second World War - so first a brief look at those churches which were built in the early years of the century, some where there was not one previously and others to cater for the growing populations of towns like Watford, St.Albans, Harpenden and later, the first Garden City at Letchworth.

St.Michael's, Woolmer Green (1899-1900) and St.Martin's, Preston (1900) appear to fit the first requirement - although it seems strange at Preston, the home of the Knights Templars and Hospitallers at Temple Dinsley - whilst Christ Church in the St.Albans Road (1904) and The United Reformed Church in Clarendon Road (1903) joined St.John the Evangelist Church in Sutton Road (completed 1893) to make a trio of new churches in Watford either in the last decade of the 19th or in the first of the 20th century. St.Saviour's (1902) and St.Paul's (1910) added to the number of churches in St.Albans whilst at Harpenden no fewer than four churches were built over a period of 30 years: The United Reformed Church (1897), St.John the Baptist Church (1908), The Methodist Church in the High Street (1929) and finally the Roman Catholic Church of Our Lady of Lourdes was begun in 1928 and completed in 1936 by F.A.Walters who, earlier, had done some work at St.Edmund's College at Old Hall Green.

When the first Garden City was started in 1903, the churches in the three original villages - Norton, Willian and Letchworth - formed a nucleus of old churches but as Letchworth grew so did the demand for more places of worship for different denominations. The Official Guide states that " As well as seven Anglican churches, Letchworth houses 13 Nonconformist churches and the Roman Catholic and Liberal Catholic churches of St.Hugh and St.Alban." This list includes, of course, the three old churches in the seven Anglican churches whilst several others were built between the wars with "Howgills", the Friends' Meeting House, being built as early as 1907. This pattern was reflected, to a certain extent, in Welwyn Garden City and, in the post-war years, in the New Towns.

Whilst the first Garden City was growing in Letchworth, with "Howgills" the only new place of worship to be built before the First World War, another new church was being constructed in Knebworth in 1914 by the fashionable architect Sir Edwin Lutyens - arguably the earliest unorthodox shape in the county. The old village of Knebworth had possessed St.Mary and St.Thomas Church for centuries but it was in the grounds of Knebworth House and a long way from the small town which had grown up around the A1 south of Stevenage (Now the B197): Pevsner considers that St.Martin's Church is "One of Lutyens most remarkable churches" but, of the three bays of the nave, only one was built by him in 1914, whilst the rest was completed by Sir Albert Richardson as late as 1963-4. Another tale of protracted building is that of what is now the All Saints Pastoral Centre at London Colney although it was originally an Anglican Convent. Begun in 1899, the chapel was not added until 1927 and was extended, following the original designs, in 1964 and is now much admired from the fast-moving (or otherwise) traffic on the M25 Motorway!

Hertfordshire - as in the 17th century - again escaped wholesale destruction of churches during the Second World War but with the growth of the New Towns and expanding populations there was the need for new churches in the aftermath. Not all of these churches were unusual - some were conventional in appearance and certainly so from the outside - but several, mentioned very early on in this book, were "out of the ordinary" and so deserve to be listed here but with fuller details in the Gazetteer. St.George's Church, Stevenage (1956) - the one which Pevsner called "depressingly ugly" - St.John's Church, at the Hilltop, Hatfield (1960-2), All Saints, Harpenden (1961-2) and St.Andrew's Church at Cuffley (1965) together with The Free Church nearby, are all somewhat out of the norm.

St. George's Church, Letchworth (1961-4) with its tall concrete spire is a particularly impressive design and vies only with St. Andrew's at Cuffley in its spectacular siting.

Three more places of worship will close this chapter, not only on post-war building but also on the whole period from the Reformation, with the details to be found in The Gazetteer. St. Bartholemew The Apostle, St. Albans (1962-4) brought a second Roman Catholic church to the City, The Church of the Seventh-Day Adventists brought a new shape to St. Albans whilst a new faith in the area is exemplified by the little Jamia Mosque situated on the edge of the Ring Road at Watford..

CHAPTER FIVE

WHAT TO LOOK FOR INSIDE A CHURCH

The comment was made early on that this book was basically intended for the curious layman - rather than for the expert - but information about the various artefacts, fittings, monuments, woodwork, wall paintings etc., etc., will be of help to all those for like to visit old churches and examine them with some prior knowledge even if they are not delving deeply into church history. Not all of the fitments will be found in every church - certainly not in the modern ones and, of course, many objects disappeared not only during the "Reformation" but also during the heavy-handed "restorations" of the 19th century - but these descriptions will, I hope, add to a visitor's pleasure when making a tour of any of the county's churches. The descriptions will cover objects both large and small but The Glossary contains further information which includes architectural technical terms.

In some churches the visitor will find small guide books - often by a local historian or even by the incumbent - or, perhaps, only a gen sheet in portable form for use just whilst inspecting the building: unfortunately, often there is nothing, but, whether there is any guide or not, remember that churches need upkeep and a little donation, however small, will help to relieve the heavy drain on parish resources.

ALMS BOXES or CHESTS -- Many churches today have small wall safes for any donations towards their upkeep - these safes being, unfortunately, most necessary in the late twentieth century because of the ever present danger of theft from those churches which endeavour to stay open during the day - but this was not always so although it was the "poor" who were the main recipients, in the past, of the contents of the boxes or chests to be found in the county. The 1st Poor Law Act of 1552 enacted that collections were to be made in each parish for the poor but it was the later Poor Law of Elizabeth 1st in 1601 which proclaimed that each parish was responsible for its own paupers: not only did this Law levy a rate on each household for the purpose but the provision of a box for offerings was also ordered.

At Cheshunt - where they were ahead of even the first Poor Law - the clergy were ordered in 1547 to " provide a strong chest with a hole in the upper part thereof, having three keys: which chest you shall set and fasten near unto the high altar, to the intent the parishioners should put into it their oblation and alms for their poor neighbours." This chest, with a slit in the lid to receive coins, can still be seen in St.Mary's Church.   Alms chests can be seen at Albury, Bishops Stortford, Kings Walden, Pirton, and in several other churches. In the south aisle of the presbytery of the Cathedral there is a poor box of circa 1650 and on the wall above is a little wooden man holding out his hat for alms.

ALTAR -- From the 7th to the 16th centuries, churches were primarily just shelters for altars and were made of stone: but after the Reformation they were usually made of wood with some Elizabethan and Jacobean Communion tables being very finely carved. The High Altar is the central point of a church and, since the edict of Archbishop Laud in the reign of Charles I, it should be kept permanently at the east end and enclosed by rails at which communicants can kneel.   Altars today are are usually hidden by the normal three linen cloths - changed according to the season of the Church year - so it is difficult to know of what they are made but, at least, there can be no problem in locating the altar at the east end of every church. There is just one exception to this almost universal rule: the orientation of the "New" Ayot St.Lawrence Church is the reverse of what is customary with the altar being at the *west* end.

ALTAR TOMB or TOMB CHEST -- Modern terms for a tomb of stone or marble resembling an altar - but not used as such - and usually with an effigy of a nobleman and, sometimes, with his wife and family. There are many such tombs in the county churches and some of the oldest are at Benington, Anstey, Eastwick and Little Munden.   In St.John the Baptist Church at Aldbury there is an elaborate tomb with the effigies of Sir Robert Whittingham and his wife: his feet rest on what is known as the "wild man". Although there are more decorative mural monuments incorporating altar tombs, one of the most decorative altar tombs - without an effigy - is that of Edmund of Langley, the son of Edward III, in the north aisle of All Saints Church, Kings Langley.

APSE -- A rarity in Hertfordshire. The semi-circular or polygonal end of a chancel or other part of a church. There are Norman apses at Bengeo, Great Amwell and Great Wymondley whilst an apse was added as recently as 1899 to St.Peter's Church in Buntingford. There is an architectural curiosity at St.Mary Magdalene, Offley, where the chancel was recased and refitted in the late 18th century: it is apsidal inside but square outside.

ARMOUR -- Many of the effigies lying on top of altar tombs are "dressed" in beautifully carved reproductions - in wood, alabaster or bronze - of armour and these are very useful aids for the study of medieval armour and costume. In some chapels may be found pieces of armour - particularly gauntlets and helmets: Sir Ralph Sadleir died in 1587 and by his monument in St.Mary's Church, Standon, are two helmets, sword, spurs etc.

AUMBRIES -- Recesses in the chancel wall to hold the sacred vessels for Mass and Communion together with the three holy oils used for Baptism, Confirmation and for the anointing the sick when they were very ill. The Royal Commission lists these and other "cupboards" under the generic title of LOCKERS so enabling larger recesses to be included which were used to hold processional crosses and banners: one such, measuring 12ft by 1ft8in, is at Kelshall. Smaller recesses - which originally would have had wooden doors - can be seen at Aldbury (where the recess is mentioned in the guide), Bushey (St.James), Clothall, Ippollitts and some other churches.

BENCH ENDS -- In the early days there were no seats for the congregation although in some churches there were simple benches, or even a stone seat, attached to the wall for the aged and infirm: this was the origin of the phrase "the weakest go to the wall". By the end of the 15th century, however, fixed seats were universal and beautifully carved ends began to be a feature. The tops of some of these benches are elaborately carved figures of people or animals, and are known today as "poppy heads" (derived from the French "poupee" - puppet or figurehead). Some of the finest are in East Anglia but early 15th century examples are at St.Mary's, Hitchin and also at Ardeley, Bygrave, Clothall, Kimpton, Sandon and Throcking. At Little Gaddesden there are later 17th century examples.

BEQUEST BOARDS -- A board on which a charity or bequest in the Last Will and Testament of a local Nobleman or Landowner is recorded: this may be in the chancel but more often in the base of church towers. An example can be seen at the base of the tower of St.Augustine's Church, Broxbourne where Charity Boards show benefactions dating back to 1440.

BOX PEWS -- During the 17th and 18th centuries benches were replaced by enclosed seating - known today as Box Pews but, because of their appearance, they were familiarly known as "horse-boxes". This name was more particularly given to the high box pews made for the gentry (where, unseen, they often made themselves very comfortable) but, later on, smaller and lower box pews were built, in the nave, for the rest of the congregation. Most of these were removed in the 19th century - with some remaining into the present century - but at Little Hadham and at Stanstead St.Margaret, low box pews are still in position whilst at Stanstead Abbots there is a complete set of high box pews.

BRASSES -- It is said that more brasses remain in England than in the whole of Europe, and that they are more common in the south-east. There are many brasses in the county and one of the oldest is of Sir Richard Torrington and his wife in St.Peter's, Berkhamsted (1356): another is of Sir Philip Peletoot at Watton-at-Stone (1361). The brasses in the county can be dated from the 14th century right through to the 17th century but many have disappeared - some through being melted down as scrap metal but for very little reward - so if you wish to take a "rubbing", it is usual to pay a fee after first obtaining permission.

BUSTS -- Full-length effigies are to be seen in many churches but Busts of deceased worthies - usually in niches - are somewhat rare. There are two busts of outstanding quality in oval niches in St.Mary's, Monken Hadley dating from 1616 whilst other busts may be found in the churches at Ardeley, Braughing, Meesden, Willian and Wyddial.

CANOPIES -- see TESTERS

CAPITALS -- The top or cap of a pillar or column from which an arch springs: they are included here as well as in the Glossary because many of them are richly carved with human, animal or floral designs and well worth taking a look at for the sheer ingenuity of the medieval masons' work. There are fine capitals with floral designs of circa 1230 in St.Mary Magdalene Church, Offley but many other finely moulded examples can be found throughout the county.

<u>CARTOUCHE TABLETS</u> -- Wall tablets with an ornate frame and, although usually of marble, look like scrolls enclosing an inscription. There is a finely designed cartouche, containing an epitaph on the life of John Halsey who died in 1670, in the chancel at Great Gaddesden: this is surmounted by a bust.

<u>CHANCEL</u> -- That part of the East end of a church in which the altar is placed, and separated from the nave by a screen - should there still be one - although those remaining are just reminders of the past.

<u>CHANCEL ARCHES</u> -- The arch spanning the west end of the chancel, or, more practically, the arch between the chancel and the nave. Most medieval churches have a chancel arch - from where the "Chancel Screen" was removed - but exceptionally fine 13th century arches are still in place at St.Botolph's, Eastwick and St.Mary's, Standon where it is enriched by "dogtooth" ornament of circa 1230.

<u>CHANCEL SCREENS</u> also called <u>ROOD SCREENS</u> -- In medieval times, the chancel (see above) was reserved for the priest and the nave for the congregation: the screen, with locked doors, was used to keep "the people" and dogs away from the chancel. The screens were usually of finely carved wood, although sometimes of stone, and were surmounted by a loft or platform: over this , supported by it or a separate beam, stood the Rood which was an image of Christ on the Cross and supported by images of the Virgin Mary and St.John the Evangelist on either side. The loft was approached by a staircase, either of wood or in a turret built into the wall, but although some staircases can still be seen along with an opening in the chancel arch, not a single loft has been preserved in the county. Most of the Roods were swept away at the Reformation and their final removal, along with the lofts, was ordained in 1561. Many medieval screens, however, have been preserved and the oldest is at St.Mary's, Gilston: there are two others of note dating from the 15th century at Kimpton and Redbourn (here dated by a bequest of 1478). The unique 14th century stone screen at Sandridge was mentioned in chapter 3 but do not overlook what Pevsner calls the "gorgeous, if decidedly worldly" chancel screen which was erected when the

chancel of All Saints, St.Paul's Walden, was remodelled in 1727.

CHANTRY CHAPEL -- A small chapel usually occupying part of a large building, especially dedicated and endowed for chanting memorial Masses for the soul of the founder or his relatives.   There are a number of chapels in the aisles of parish churches in the county and some of them are very elaborate: of particular interest are The Salisbury Chapel at Hatfield, The Morison Chapel at St.Mary's, Watford and The Pendley Chapel at Aldbury (see ALTAR TOMB). The only true Chantry Chapels in the county are those of the Duke of Gloucester, Abbot Wallingford and Abbot Ramryge in the Cathedral

CHARNEL HOUSE -- A crypt or cellar in which bones removed from churchyards have been placed. Several churches in England still have a charnel house but the only one in the county is under the east bay of the chancel at St.Mary's Church, Hitchin.

CHESTS see ALMS BOXES

CHOIR STALLS -- The choir stalls to be found in many churches - built in the chancel to accomodate a "choir" as we know it today - are often comparatively modern with many only dating from the 19th century. Stalls or benches were originally provided solely for the parish priest, other clergy and, possibly, for the parish clerk: in Medieval times, when services were often very long, misericords - if installed - formed a rest for the users.   Some very early and beautifully carved stalls still survive with the earliest being the 14th century examples - with 7 contemporary misericords - at Anstey: other 14th or 15th century stalls with misericords are at Bishops Stortford and Stevenage (St.Nicholas). There is an unusual relic at All Saints, Willian where the 15th century stalls have been cleared away from the chancel: three of the original bench ends have been made up into a large chair with two of the "poppyheads" being an elephant and a carving of John The Baptist's head on a charger - both extraordinary examples of the 15th century woodcarver's art.

COFFIN LIDS or SLABS -- In the 12th and 13th centuries stone coffins were being used for those of eminence or wealth, with some of them being buried in the floor of the church so that the lids of the coffins formed part of the floor. It is very unlikely that the bodies are still buried in the churches but a number of coffin lids - often decorated with a foliated Cross - can be seen (if not covered by a carpet) in the county. There are 13th century slabs at Gilston, Sarratt and Tring, whilst 14th century slabs can be found at Aldenham, Berkhamsted, Furneux Pelham, Hinxworth and at St.Michael's in St.Albans.

COMMANDMENT BOARDS -- It was following the Reformation, when churches appeared bare after being stripped of their Roman Catholic associations, that panels showing the Ten Commandments, The Lord's Prayer and the Creed were first put up to remedy this and for the edification of the congregation. It is obvious that many guides fail to mention that there are Commandment Boards on the walls in a church but, if in position above the altar or elsewhere, they cannot be overlooked even if some are nearly illegible. One of the oldest (1627) is at St.Lawrence, Abbots Langley whilst others can be found at Brent Pelham, Essendon and Great Gaddesden.

COMMUNION TABLES -- (see also ALTARS) The Communion Tables, which replaced the stone altars after the Reformation, were moved in many instances to the middle of the chancel, but altars today, as has already been remarked upon earlier, are, as a general rule, situated at the east end of the church. I am unable to say whether any of the altars in the county contain original tables but some two dozen 17th century Communion Tables are still to be found: Baldock (in the north chapel), Benington (in the chapel behind the organ) and Ware (in the south chapel) are just three of the churches possessing them and where they are being put to a different use.

CORBEL -- A projecting stone or piece of timber supporting, or intended to support, some horizontal feature such as a beam or an arch. This is another architectural device included here as well as in the Glossary because those of the 13th and 15th centuries gave the stone-masons an opportunity to show their skill and imagination in carving. There are many fantastic heads, often grotesque albeit amusing at the same time, so do not fail to glance upwards in the nave of those churches where they are to be found and the details are in the Gazetteer. A particular good example is St.Michael's, Bishops Stortford where the guide draws attention to the corbels: "The Corbels in the North and South aisles repay a close examination. They represent angels and rustic characters, some with their tools and others with animal faces".

CREDENCE -- A shelf or table on which the vessels for Mass were placed before being consecrated. This was often a slab of wood or stone inserted into the actual piscina recess above the bowl. Credences, of the 13th or 14th centuries, built into piscinae are to be seen at Gilston, Ippollitts and Much Hadham whilst a 12th century credence, discovered in the tower during 19th century restorations, is now in the chancel at Widford. An unusual fitting is to be found at the new church of All Saints (1882) in Long Marston near Tring: the church includes many details from the old church (of which only the tower now remains) and one of these is a 14th century piscina with a credence in the south wall of the chancel.

DOG-TOOTH DECORATION -- Mainly Early English (13th century) decoration or ornament, consisting of four-cornered stars, found round piscinae, arches and windows: once again an architectural device is included here as well as in the Glossary. Probably the most elaborate example of dog-tooth decoration is the elaborate carving round the arches of the triforium - including the string course beneath - on the south side of the nave in The Cathedral. Dog-tooth ornamentation can be seen on the piscina and a tomb-recess at Ardeley and on a piscina at Hertingfordbury, whilst the chancel arch in St.Mary's, Standon is much enhanced because of it (see CHANCEL ARCHES).

DOLE CUPBOARD -- In medieval times, bread - bought by money from generous persons - was given to the poor in the form of a "dole" at the end of the Sunday service: the cupboard was used to keep the bread in it until it was needed. These are very rare now but in the south transept of The Cathedral is a recess containing three cupboards, dating from a charity of 1628, which used to be filled with bread on a saturday night ready for the next "dole".

DOOM PAINTING -- In medieval days the interior walls of churches were covered in paintings and usually there was one depicting the Day of Judgement - a painting showing what might happen to evil-doers at the last trump: these were very "awesome" and frightening because they were intended to convince the usually illiterate congregations to mend their ways. These paintings are known as "Dooms" and the only one known to exist in the county - and that only part of a 15th century one - is now on the south wall of the nave of St.Michael's Church, St.Albans.

<u>DOORS</u> -- It goes without saying that there is at least one door into every church but, in several, doors of great antiquity have been preserved with some of them still being put to good use. The 14th century wooden door, with its long iron hinges, is still in use in the south porch at Clothall and here also notice the name of "John Warrin" - the craftsman who made it - inscribed on the side facing into the nave: at Brent Pelham the original traceried 14th century south door is preserved alongside the new although this is in the porch. Two even older doors are at Little Hormead where its north door, with its lavish 12th century ironwork and various interlacing patterns on it, is preserved in the blocked north doorway: the other is at Much Hadham where there is an oak door to the vestry which has good early 13th century ironwork.

<u>EASTER SEPULCHRES</u> -- A recess in the north wall of the chancel (or a canopied tomb used for the purpose): on Good Friday, in medieval days, the Host and an altar crucifix were placed in the Sepulchre and then watched over, day and night, until they were removed, with much ceremony, to the high altar very early on Easter morning. Most have disappeared now but they can be seen at Furneux Pelham and Sandon, whilst at Ardeley and Much Hadham there are tomb recesses in the chancel which were used for the purpose.

<u>EFFIGIES</u> -- (see also <u>ALTAR TOMB</u>) There are a number of sepulchral monuments or effigies lying on top of altar tombs, ranging from the 13th to the 16th century, and prior to the Reformation, effigies were carved in a reverent attitude with hands folded in prayer: in the 17th century, however, some effigies were depicted leaning on an elbow or kneeling. Round the sides of some tombs there may be effigies of all the children of the deceased - in order of their age and size - and these are known as "weepers". The oldest effigy in the county is at Eastwick where the marble figure of a knight, in complete chain mail together with a long shield, is dated 13th century: it is so well carved that, along with others similar, it forms a valuable example for the study of medieval armour. In complete contrast to this is the life-size marble figure of Sir Francis Bacon, who died in 1626, and who is depicted seated upright, apparently comfortably asleep, in a niche by the altar of St.Michael's Church, St.Albans!

<u>FAMILY PEWS</u> -- Pews which were set aside for the Lord of the Manor etc., apart from "the people" and often comfortably furnished, sometimes even with a fireplace! After the Reformation, in some instances, chantry enclosures became Family Pews: the only obvious example still to be seen in the county is at St.Dunstan's Church, Hunsdon, where a fine Jacobean oak screen was erected between the south chapel - in which are Cary memorials and the Family Pews - and the nave.

<u>FONTS</u> -- All churches have a font for the purpose of Baptism and there are a surprising number of medieval examples still in use - some carved with weird beasts or figures - even though many of the churches where they can be found have otherwise been entirely rebuilt. Exceptional examples of carved fonts are at St.George's Church, Anstey (12th century) and at St.Mary's Church, Ware (14th century). There is another interesting one, dated circa 1420, at Widford: it is octagonal with sides panelled and carved with various subjects - the head of a lion, a nun, etc.

<u>FURNITURE</u> -- CHAIRS -- A single heavy-looking chair may often be seen in churches against the north wall of the chancel - even within the altar rails - and this will be for the use of the diocesan Bishop when visiting the church. There is nothing very special about most of them but a few are very old and, consequently, are of special interest: at Much Hadham there are two chairs of circa 1400 which were formerly part of a sedilia and at The Oxhey Chapel there is an elaborately carved chair of the 16th century. Do not forget the chair at Willian which was made up from choir stalls.
      DESKS (see also <u>PULPITS</u>) -- During 19th century restorations at Royston, a 15th century parclose screen (one between a chapel and the body of the church) was discovered but the guide book tells us that it was "then unfortunately hacked up to make the present pulpit and clergy desks". At All Saints, St.Paul's Walden there is a desk and a Bible-Box of the 17th century.

<u>GALLERY</u> -- After the Restoration of Charles II, and particularly when Wren was rebuilding the churches of the City of London after the Great Fire, some churches built galleries at the west end of the nave - these were either for the use of musicians or, as Wren put it when describing his new churches --they were added to "a building in which all the congregation could conveniently see and hear the minister". There is no evidence that there were very many in the

county although there is still one in the west transept, with plain
Ionic columns, which is contemporary with the building of St.Peter's,
Buntingford.

GLASS -- There is stained glass in most churches although much
of it today is of the 19th century. Stained glass windows added
glorious colour to many medieval churches but, because of destruction after the Reformation, there are only comparatively few fragments remaining: 14th century at Buckland, Clothall and Offley
whilst at Little Hadham, Much Hadham and a few other churches
there are some more complete 15th century remains. An oddity
among stained glass windows is what is known as a "Jesse Window"
- one which shows the genealogy tree of Jesus Christ - and the
remains of a 14th century one in the south aisle at St.Mary
Magdalene, Barkway is believed to be the only one in the county.
By the 19th century, the art of glass painting had sunk to a low ebb
but by the end of the century the Pre-Raphaelites under William
Morris and Edward Burne-Jones had left a completely different
legacy. There are fine examples of their work at St.Michael's,
Waterford and at St.Mary's, Furneux Pelham.

GRAFFITI -- A graffito is defined by the "Shorter Oxford English
Dictionary" as "A drawing or writing scratched on a wall or other
surfaces, as at Pompeii and Rome". The purpose of some of these
graffiti is not always clear nor can they always be accurately dated
but there are a few churches, together with the Cathedral, where
interesting examples of graffiti can be seen. Both the church at
Anstey and St.Nicholas Church, Stevenage, contain several examples each, but, probably the best known place in the county to see
graffiti of the 14th century is at Ashwell. Not only is there a
remarkably detailed and accurate scratching of Old St.Paul's Cathedral but there are a series of writings in Latin bemoaning the
outbreak of the Black Death - together with some personal comments on local people!

GRILLE -- A screen of wrought iron used to protect a tomb. The
only example in the county is that already described in the chapter
on the Cathedral - the Iron Grille separating Duke Humphrey's
Chantry from the south aisle.

HAGIOSCOPES see SQUINTS

HATCHMENTS -- A display of a coat-of-arms or the family crest on a lozenge-shaped frame, usually of wood: these boards, some four or five feet square, were introduced towards the end of the 17th century. They would first be carried in the funeral procession and then, after being displayed for some months on the house of the deceased, they would be fixed permanently in the church. There are many heraldic devices with shields in brass, iron, stone and wood in the county but hatchments have to be searched for. Favourite spots to find them are over the north and south doors - as with those at St.Michael's Church, Bishops Stortford.

HOUR-GLASSES -- Hour-glasses (filled with sand and so very similar to modern egg-timers) were introduced in the 16th century for the purpose of timing sermons, and became in general use in the 17th century. They were usually fitted into wrought-iron stands, but there are now only just three of these stands to be found in the county: at Bygrave, Sacombe and at St.Michael's Church, St.Albans.

IRONWORK -- (see also DOORS and GRILLE) The decorated iron door-hinges at Little Hormead and at Clothall have already been mentioned above but there is more 12th century iron scroll work at Codicote. 13th century work can be found on the south door at St.Mary's Church, the original little church at Letchworth, whilst at Widford there is 13th century work on both the south door and on the vestry door. 15th century locks, handles or keys are still in use at Kelshall and St.John's Church, Barnet.

JESSE WINDOW -- see GLASS

LECTERNS -- The Lectern is used to hold the open Bible for the reading of the Scriptures and often made up in the form of an eagle with out-stretched wings. Today Lecterns are usually made of brass but in medieval times they were carved out of wood: the only wooden example left in the county is at St. John the Baptist Church, Aldbury.

MISERICORDS -- (see also CHOIR STALLS) A projecting bracket - usually carved with quaint figures - affixed to the underside of the seat of a stall so that when the seat, which is hinged, is turned up against the back, the bracket forms a rest for the user. It appears that the wood-carvers of these misericords - usually of the 13th, 14th and 15th centuries - were given a lot of freedom in using their imagination because many of the carvings are amusing and grotesque. Surprisingly, although there are many to be found in other Cathedrals, there are none in St.Albans but there are misericords to be found in the three parish churches of Anstey, Bishops Stortford and at St.Nicholas, Stevenage.

MONUMENTS and MEMORIALS -- Some of the oldest monuments have been discussed above under ALTAR TOMB and EFFIGIES, but there are many more dating from circa 1300 to the beginning of the 18th century. After the Reformation there was a change in style, and again after the Restoration of Charles II in 1660 when many more mural memorials were put up - often extolling only the virtues of the deceased in flowery language with miniature figures kneeling on either side of the tablet. I will mention just two Monuments here - one at the beginning of the 17th century and the other after the Restoration. The Salisbury Chapel in St.Etheldreda's Church, Hatfield was built in 1618 by William, the 2nd Earl of Salisbury, to hold the tomb of his father - Robert Cecil, the 1st Earl of Salisbury and the builder of Hatfield House. The other is one of what Pevsner calls "the most sumptuous series of monuments in the county" in the Church of St.Mary and St.Thomas in the grounds of Knebworth House. These are the monuments to the Lytton family with the more than life-size figure of Mr.Lytton Lytton, who died in 1710, being the most prominent.

PAINTINGS -- see WALL PAINTINGS

PARCLOSE SCREENS -- These are screens which separate a chapel from the rest of the church: they are made of stone - which is uncommon - or of wood. There is a fine 15th century stone screen around the Pendley Chapel and the monument to Sir Richard Whittingham at Aldbury whilst there is a complete set of wooden screens at St.Nicholas, Stevenage.

PEWS -- see BOX PEWS and FAMILY PEWS All churches have pews of some type or another but a special mention must be made here of St.Mary's Church, Hertingfordbury: in the restoration of 1891, new benches were carved by Josef Mayer of Oberammergau, who had played the part of Christ in the Passion Play. The little, but very informative, church guide tells us that he was invited to England by Lord Cowper of Panshanger to undertake this work: Mayer carved his signature on the first pew.

PISCINAE -- A piscina is a basin with a drain, set in a niche or recess in the wall south of an altar, for washing the Communion or Mass vessels: sometimes ornamented in the same period style as the doorways or arches of the church concerned. If a piscina is seen in a wall other than as part of the chancel, it is likely that an altar stood there at some time in the church's history. Although normally not now in use, there are a number of piscinae to be found in medieval churches and some have interesting ornamentation: the dogtooth decoration at Ardeley has already been mentioned above and there is a crocketted canopy over the piscina at Wheathampstead but fuller details are in the Gazetteer. (see also CREDENCE)

PULPITS -- One always takes it for granted that there will be a pulpit in a church but - although there were pre-Reformation pulpits with those at Graveley and Much Hadham being made up from 14th or 15th century remnants - it was only in 1603 that wardens were ordered to provide pulpits where none existed previously. Some of these early 17th century pulpits were very elaborately carved and have become known as "Jacobean": the pulpits at Kings Langley and at St.Michael's Church, St.Albans - both with "testers" or sounding boards - are particularly good examples. After the Restoration what is known as the "three-decker" pulpit came into use because of the high box pews: there were three levels with the pulpit proper at the top, the lectern at the next level and finally, at the lowest or pew level, was the clerk who read the responses. These were mostly swept away during the 19th century restorations but, in the county, Little Hadham and St.James Church, Stanstead Abbots have still retained these fittings: it is to be hoped that future "restorers" will not remove these links with the past.

REREDOSES -- Technically a reredos is the whole of the space between the top of the altar and the window-sill, or a wall or screen of stone or wood at the back of the altar containing, possibly, panels of The Commandments and The Creed, but, for the purposes of this book, look for painted or carved panels just above the altar. First, however, two medieval survivors. A 14th century reredos of seven stone canopied niches was discovered walled up during restorations in 1865 at St.Helen's Church, Wheathampstead and this is now installed below the east window in the north transept: the other is at the east end of the south aisle of St.Nicholas Church, Great Munden where there is a 15th century stone reredos, consisting of five trefoiled niches with ogee heads, with a castellated top.

Apart from the Cathedral reredos, already described in chapter 2, there are interesting comparatively modern examples at Hertingfordbury (1891) and at Kings Langley (1878) and in both of these marble or alabaster figures have been carved in relief.

ROOD SCREENS -- see CHANCEL SCREENS

SEDILIA -- Alongside the piscina, and sometimes built as one unit with it, was a set of recessed seats: in the 13th century they were usually in line whereas in the 14th century they were of different heights with the priest being nearest the altar. In the 15th century they appear to be back on one level, but after that there do not seem to be any more built. The sedilia at Benington, Furneux Pelham and Walkern are all of the 13th century whilst there are 14th century sedilia at Ashwell, Sandon, and a few other places including Baldock where the piscina and the sedilia form a group.

SQUINTS (also called HAGIOSCOPES) -- A squint is an aperture pierced through a wall to allow the view of an altar from places - e.g. a chantry in an aisle - whence it would otherwise be hidden. There are squints at Anstey, Great Wymondley, Standon and, particularly obvious, a pair with rounded heads at Great Amwell. There was one at Watton-at-Stone but this is now blocked off.

STAIRWAY TO ROOD LOFT -- (see CHANCEL SCREENS) The Roods and Rood Lofts were all swept away after 1561 but some of the staircases which lead to the Rood Lofts have remained along with their doorways. Openings can be seen at several churches in the county near the chancel arch and, in some instances, the staircase itself. Some of these staircases have remained because they were built into the thickness of the wall - as at Great Wymondley where both doorways also remain: both doorways can also be seen at Hunsdon, Norton and Thorley.

STOUPS -- Recessed basins, placed in the porch or just inside the church door, containing consecrated or "holy water": all who entered the church used to dip their finger in and make the sign of the Cross on their foreheads and breast to remind them of the frailty of human life etc -- "unstable as water". The only remains of stoups inside churches are at Albury, Broxbourne, Buckland, Tewin and Thorley.

TESTERS or SOUNDING BOARDS -- A horizontal board or canopy over a pulpit to help carry the preacher's voice to the far end of the church.   Only the Little Hadham "three-decker" pulpit retains its tester - it is missing from the other one at Stanstead Abbots - but there are several testers still remaining elsewhere: the "Jacobean" pulpits at Kings Langley and St.Michael's Church, St.Albans both have testers.   There are also testers still in place at Bushey and Sarratt.

WALL PAINTINGS -- A description of the nave and other paintings in the Cathedral has already been given in chapter 2 but Hertford-shire can boast of some spectacular examples of clerical wall paintings in country churches - the surviving remains of drawings which, in medieval times, covered the walls as a means of bringing the story of The Bible to the unlettered peasants.   All this was changed at the Reformation and attempts were made then, and later by the Puritans, to dispense with this so-called "popish idolatry." Some were physically hacked away but, because the cheapest and quickest way was to cover them with coatings of whitewash, a few have been discovered underneath the whitewash, been cleaned up and are now are precious relics of the past.   The most prolific paintings, and what Pevsner has labelled as "Apart from St.Albans, the most important series in the county ", are in St.Leonard's Church, Flamstead, but look for them also in the churches at Abbots Langley, Bengeo, Cottered, Kimpton and Widford.

CHAPTER SIX

WHAT TO SEE OUTSIDE CHURCHES

In the last chapter the various fittings and furnishings to be found inside a church have been listed and , I hope, explained but, as the visitor may have entered the building without pausing in the churchyard, this chapter will deal with what can be seen *outside* after leaving the church once again: at the same time the general fabric of the building or "Turriform", including the porches , will be described.

In some counties the parish church is not sited near the village - possibly hidden away in trees or in the grounds of the former Lord of the Manor - but in Hertfordshire, however, this is not so except in rare cases: for example, the little church at Meesden, in the north-eastern corner of the county, lies away from the village whilst St.Mary and St.Thomas Church is in the grounds of Knebworth House. In most villages, the church is in the middle of the houses and complete with a graveyard: in towns, however, the graveyard may have disappeared although the little churchyard of St.Mary's Church, Watford, is a haven of rest virtually in the middle of a very bustling town.

It is of interest to note that the church of St.Bartholemew at Layston - a mile or so east of Buntingford - was neglected and finally closed as recently as 1951 after the population of the village had, by the end of the middle ages, moved to where the trade was, on Ermine Street (now the A10): Buntingford grew, built its own church of St.Peter (see chapter 4) and Layston became a "Deserted Village".

When looking at the exterior of the churches in Hertfordshire there is one feature which, above all, helps to single out the county churches from those elsewhere: this is known as The Hertfordshire Spike. Not universal by any means but a number of the sturdy towers, which are often battlemented, carry short but slender spirelets which are known locally by this soubriquet: another name used is the "snuffer". The central tower of the Cathedral originally had a spire but this was replaced by a "spike" which can be seen in some of the old prints.   It was removed, according to Pevsner, in 1832.   It should be pointed out that the use of the "spike" is not confined to medieval towers: the Roman Catholic Church of St.Bartholemew The Apostle on Watling Street in St.Albans, built in 1964, can truly boast that it has carried on the tradition of the Hertfordshire Spike!

APSE -- Listed already under "What to Look for inside a Church", I have included the item again in this chapter - not only because they are rare in this county - but because it is so easy to view the three Norman apses at Bengeo, Great Amwell and Great Wymondley, from the churchyard thus getting a complete view of each building as a whole entity.

BEDHEAD GRAVEBOARDS see GRAVEBOARDS

BELLCOTES or BELL TURRETS -- Bells are normally housed in church towers and their purpose is to summon people to worship: such bells are heavy but in a small church without tower or spire, much smaller bells are housed in an open bellcote which is usually gabled and on top of the main roof.   Their purpose, of course, remains the same.   Two examples are St.Leonard's at Bengeo where a bellcote was added in the 19th century to the Norman building, and the other is St.Peter's at Buntingford, completed in 1626 with a contemporary bellcote.

CLOCKS -- In medieval times there were "clock-jacks" - ingen- iously devised automatic figures - to give the time (and a few of these survive in East Anglia) but it was not until the 17th century that dialled clocks began to appear on village church towers.   There is no point in listing those churches with clocks and those without, but, take a look up at the tower before leaving and you will find that some of the clocks are of more than passing interest.   Particularly note Furneux Pelham with its message underneath --"Mind Your Busi- ness" -- and the fancifully designed face in a shade of blue of the clock on St.Peter's Church, Ayot St.Peter.

CORBEL TABLES -- The phrase "Corbel Table" is applied to the use of corbels on the exterior of a building - in effect, it is usually a row of corbels supporting some projecting masonry and particularly a sloping projecting roof to throw rain clear of the walls. As with the interior types, many of these corbels were carved with quaint heads or figures.   A corbel table can be seen the whole length of the embattled parapet of the south aisle of St.Mary's Church, Redbourn and at Meesden, with its porch completely of brick of circa 1530, where there is a corbel table over the archway contemporary with the porch.

CORPSE-GATE see LYCH-GATE

CROSSES -- Before the Reformation, every churchyard had a cross in it - erected to the south of the church to denote that it was consecrated ground. The cross was an important "station" in the Palm Sunday processions and was sometimes used for public announcements. Few remain in the county but the bases of just two crosses can be seen in the churchyards of Great Munden and Kelshall - and here it has been converted into a sundial. The village of Kelshall is somewhat unique in that it has also the remains of another cross of the 14th century which was unearthed locally in 1906: this is now set up on a patch of grass between the village and the Church of St.Faith.

DOORWAYS -- In the last chapter, doors, and particularly the inside of doors, were described but it is the doorways themselves- inside porches and the actual openings in the (usually) south wall of the church - which are dealt with here and some hide most interesting architectural features or sculptures.   When visiting churches, take note of the doorway as you enter - some will be quite plain but each will be slightly different - and so comparisons can be made.   Particular note should be taken of St.James's Church, Thorley, - just south of Bishops Stortford - where a Norman 12th century chevron or "zigzag" decoration over the south doorway is concealed from the casual observer by a 19th century porch. Back in Bishops Stortford itself, the north porch of St.Michael's Church - which still has its original roof and door of the early 15th century - shelters the north doorway into the church whose spandrels (that is, the triangular-shaped spaces between the top of the arch and the doorposts) are carved with the figures of angels with a trumpet.

FLECHE -- The French word for an "arrow" but one which, like so many, has gone into the language: it is a slender spirelet which is shaped like an arrow head and placed on the roof. There is a Fleche on St.Mary's Church at Bayford and on St.John the Evangelist, Watford - both churches built in the last quarter of the 19th century.

It is important to note that, although another word for "fleche" is "spirelet", it has no connection with the "Hertfordshire Spike".

GARGOYLES -- Rainwater spouts projecting from church towers or the parapet of walls so that rainwater is thrown clear of roofs: many are carved in the form of dragons or grotesque demons and today we can enjoy the medieval craftsmen's sense of humour. There are very good medieval gargoyles at St.John the Baptist, Great Gaddesden and at All Saints, Willian: surprisingly, however, there are also dragon gargoyles on the tower of St.John's, Lemsford - a church which was only built in the middle of the last century - and they channel the rain down just like on cathedrals and medieval churches built many centuries earlier.

GRAVEBOARDS -- There are churchyards where all the above-ground evidence of burials has been removed - although sometimes the headstones have been preserved by arranging them in neat rows around the perimeters - but, in the main, the county's churches still have full churchyards and, in a few, Graveboards, or "Bedhead Graveboards" because of their shape, can be seen. These grave-boards were a cheap wooden substitute for stone and so, accordingly, were liable to crumble away unless looked after and preserved. Two which have been preserved, with interesting inscriptions, can be seen in the churchyards at Baldock and Codicote whilst others can be found at Datchworth, Graveley, Sandon , Weston and at a few other places - but mostly without inscriptions and in varying states of decay.

GRAVE COVERS -- In the second half of the 18th century, body-snatchers were very active on behalf of certain members of the medical profession so various means were devised to thwart their lucrative activities. Some graves appear completely covered from top to bottom with solid cement whilst others had a heavy iron grille over the grave with the headstone placed on top of the grille. I know of no grave in the county with such a grille but cement grave covers can be seen at Datchworth, Digswell, Great Amwell and quite an elaborate one at Newnham.

GRAVESTONES or HEADSTONES -- Their purpose was - and still is - to display inscriptions giving details of deceased people. Very few headstones earlier than the 17th century remain and they will always be found on the south side of the church: it was a common belief that the north side of the church was associated with the Devil and at the same time they did not want the shadow of the church falling on their graves.   These old headstones were often carved with the classical emblems of mortality - skulls, crossbones, hour-glasses ("the sands of time run out fast") and scythes (of Death the Reaper) were favourite carvings, along with winged heads of angels. There are, of course, unusual designs and, curiously enough, the churchyard of the former St.Botolph's Church - now a private dwelling although it retains its former exterior - at Shenley holds two very contrasting examples.   In the churchyard itself is a headstone over the grave of an airman of the First World War in the shape of Royal Flying Corps wings: in what is now part of the garden of the house, however, is the very simple black cover over the tomb of Nicholas Hawksmoor - buried in Shenley at his own request.

LYCH-GATES or CORPSE-GATES -- "Lych" was the old English word for a dead body, and, in olden times, it was the normal procedure at the lych-gate, a covered gateway at the entrance to the churchyard, for the coffin to pause whilst the priest read part of the burial service.   Most of those seen today are fairly modern - often dedicated in memory of a relative - and few remain earlier than the 17th century: the lych-gates at Anstey and Ashwell, however, are both of the 15th century.

MASS DIALS -- A primitive form of sundial may be found on the walls, or even within the south porch, of some medieval churches: they consist of only a few lines which have been cut directly on the stone.   Because of this they have become known as SCRATCH DIALS, but, as their prime function was to mark the time of Mass, they have also become known as MASS DIALS.   Some remains - perhaps only a few lines or the hole where the gnomon went - may be seen at Sandridge, North Mymms, Tewin and several other churches with all those known listed under their church entry in the Gazetteer.

PINNACLES -- The typical Hertfordshire church has a sturdy tower which is battlemented - possibly with a stair turret which finishes above the level of the battlements - and, of course, fitted with a "spike".   There are several churches, however, which have what Pevsner calls an "alien" look - they have pinnacles at the four corners of the tower summits in the manner of many Somerset churches.   Note particularly the medieval church at Barkway, which had the tower rebuilt in 1861 with pinnacles, and St.Thomas the Martyr at Northaw which was built in 1881.   Here the tower was, of course, designed with pinnacles and, in fact, there is another one on the ground which has a plaque on it which reads -- "This pinnacle belonged to the second church which stood on this site 1809-1881 when it was blown down."

PORCHES -- Most churches have a porch on the south side of the building and sometimes on the north as well - even a few on the north side only - and today it can be said that they only act as protectors of the church doorway against bad weather. In the past, however, they had many functions - at a baptism the priest commenced the service there, marriage banns were called, coroners even held court there - and the porch was one of the "stations" during church processions.   Most porches are of stone and some have a room over them - St.Mary's, Hitchin not only has a south and a north porch but both are two-storeyed - and this little room can provide a safe place for books and documents etc.   Very early porches were only of timber and there are 15th century timber porches at Hunsdon, Little Hadham and Stanstead Abbots with a brick and timber one of the same century at St.Ippollits.

RECESSED WALL TOMBS -- When walking round the outside of a church, the visitor may notice an opening in a wall - especially in very thick ones as some of the medieval walls were - and this will be the site of a recessed grave: the recess, which will have a semicircular or pointed arch over it, provided a covering for the effigy - probably long gone - which would originally have been placed there. Recesses of this type can be seen at St.Michael's Church, St.Albans and at All Saints, Willian whilst at St.Mary's Church, Watford there is, built into the west wall of the north aisle, a 14th century coffin slab with part of a cross carved on it.

RUINS and REDUNDANT CHURCHES -- St.Bartholemew's Church at Layston has already been mentioned at the beginning of this chapter so, because it seems to be the only slot suitable in the book, I will briefly bring together "Ruins" and "Redundant Churches" just to make a check list of them.   There is one other officially redundant church in the county and that is St.Mary Magdalene at Caldecote - also mentioned earlier in chapter 4 - but I will link the half-destroyed "Old" church at Ayot St.Lawrence with those two.   A

few stones remain of the original Flaunden church - on the Bucks
and Herts border and virtually inaccessible - but between Langley
and Hitchin is the 14th century Minsden Chapel.   The most
interesting ruin is that of the 14th century church of St.Etheldreda
- the only church in the county, other than Hatfield's parish church,
which is dedicated to that Saint - to be found at Chesfield a mile
down a country lane between Graveley and a north-eastern neighbourhood of Stevenage where a modern piece of sculpture has been
erected at the site to the memory of St.Etheldreda.   Finally, there
are two old church sites where just the towers remain - both hidden
away in trees: these are at Long Marston and at Thundridge.

SPIRES -- The predominant feature characteristic of many of the
county's churches is a relatively low battlemented tower - some with
a "Hertfordshire Spike" on top and a stair turret - so spires are not
at all common which makes the leaded spire of St.Mary's Church,
Hemel Hempstead so unusual: it is dated 13th century and rises to
nearly 200 feet.   Another tall spire is that at Bishops Stortford but
this one is of 1812 built on top of the 15th century tower: a somewhat
similar arrangement can be seen at Braughing where the early 15th
century tower is topped by a slender leaded spire.   The spires at
Wheathampstead and Sandridge are both out of the norm: the
tower of St.Helen's Church, Wheathampstead has an unusually
shaped broach spire which is - according to the excellent little guide
- " constructed of wood set at a very steep angle on a square base, and
rising to a diminishing octagon.   It is clad externally with strips of
lead arranged in a herringbone pattern" and this was all renewed
in 1986.   The shingled spire at Sandridge is also octagonal and
situated on top of a three-stage tower dating only from 1886.

STAIR TURRETS -- As mentioned above, one of the features of
many Hertfordshire churches is a sturdy battlemented tower complete with a stair turret and often this terminates higher than the
battlements themselves. These stair turrets are covered in and give
access to the interior of the upper stories of the tower.   Typical
examples of this can be seen at Aldenham, Berkhamsted, Broxbourne, Cheshunt, Harpenden and Weston amongst other places:
at St.Mary's, Cheshunt, the turret is surmounted by an 18th
century cupola which, until 1912, "held a bell upon which the hours
had struck for 140 years."

STOCKS -- Stocks are relics of the past when the parish had much more control over local affairs than it has today: vagrants or drunkards were often given a spell in the stocks before being sent on their way - a more serious law-breaker was sometimes held in the stocks until he could be brought before a Justice - and the custom was useful as a cheap way of dealing with trouble-makers. A few have been preserved on village greens (like at Aldbury) but in the churchyard at Great Amwell, there is a rather dilapidated set whilst at Brent Pelham, stocks, complete with a whipping post, stand just outside the gate into the churchyard.

STOUPS -- (see also the previous chapter) Recessed basins, placed in the porch or just inside the church door, containing "holy water". There are still a number of stoups to be found (some complete, some damaged) in the porches of Benington, Bishops Stortford, Furneux Pelham and others: a most elaborate unique canopied and crocketed stoup is in the porch of the redundant church at Caldecote but now probably impossible to reach.

SUNDIALS -- Not to be confused with Mass Dials, there are Sundials for telling the time (as long as the sun is out!) at Hitchin and Kelshall: there is a sundial on the tower of St.Mary's at Hitchin which was placed there in thanksgiving for the restoration of Charles II and at Kelshall a sundial has been placed on the remains of a cross in the churchyard.

TABLE TOMBS -- Altar Tombs inside a church have already been discussed but there are many to be found outside in churchyards when they are usually called "Table Tombs" - in fact, a grave raised above the level of the ground. At Great Gaddesden there is a line of five of them in the churchyard situated just below the east window, at Hertingfordbury there is an unusual one with legs at each corner and at Great Amwell there is - to quote Pevsner once again - " a Graveyard, uncommonly well provided with memorials larger than tombstones."

TOMBSTONES see GRAVESTONES

TOWERS -- The typical "sturdy embattled towers" of Hertfordshire churches have already been written about above - St.Mary's, Hitchin and St.Mary's, Redbourn fill that description more than many - but the picture would not be complete without including a few more of slightly different dimensions. The towers of two more churches dedicated to St.Mary - Ashwell and Baldock - are both taller than the average embattled towers and both have an octagonal lantern of the same pattern between the tower and a leaded spike. The height to the top of the spire at Baldock is approximately 130 feet whilst at Ashwell - with the tower itself more ambitious than any other in the county - the total height is 176 feet. One more tower must be mentioned and that is at the Church of the Holy Cross at Sarratt: here there is a short tower of the 15th century (with the top part rebuilt in the 16th century) but it is topped with a saddleback roof which is the only one in the county.

TYMPANUM -- An enclosed space between the lintel at the top of a doorway and the arc of the arch above, and, where they remain, there is usually a design or a sculpture. There is a tympanum above the medieval door in the south porch of St.Mary's Church, Hitchin and I would be glad to learn about any other tympani on the exterior of the county's churches - I know, of course, of the tympanum which separates the nave from the chancel at Bushey.

WEATHERVANES or WEATHERCOCKS -- Most churches - except possibly the very modern ones - have a weathervane or weathercock on the tower or spire, and this tradition has a very long history because there is one depicted in the Bayeux Tapestry. It is said that the cock refers to the fall of St.Peter ("Peter denied again: and immediately the cock crew." St.John chap 18. v.27) and also to intimate the necessity for watchfulness and humility. It is not always a cock which crowns the vane - sometimes it is a fish or a key but I have no record of the various devices employed in the county.

GLOSSARY OF TERMS

AISLE -- The longitudinal space usually beside and parallel to the nave or chancel.

ALTAR TOMB -- A modern term for a tomb of stone or marble resembling an altar but not used as one.

AMBULATORY -- A walkway or passageway behind the sanctuary and high altar across the east end of the church.

APSE -- Half-circular or polygonal end of a chancel - or, occasionally, another part of a church such as a transept.

ARABESQUE -- Light and fanciful ornamental strapwork for enriching flat surfaces.

ARCADE -- A succession of open or closed arches on columns or piers.

ARCH -- A structure (often carved) of stone or brick so arranged that the parts support each other by mutual pressure.

AUMBRY or AUMBREY -- A small cupboard or recess cut or built into a wall to hold the sacred vessels for Mass and Communion.

BALDACCHINO -- An ornamental canopy supported on columns - usually over an altar.

BALUSTER -- A short pillar which usually supports a hand rail - usually of fanciful outline. The term is also applied to the bulbous-looking legs of some Communion Tables of the 17th century.

BATTER -- The receding slope from the ground upwards on the vertical surface of a wall or buttress or, more simply, the inclined face of a wall.

BATTLEMENT -- The parapet of a tower or an aisle (like at Redbourn) with a series of indentations or embrasures with raised portions between. Also called castellations or crenellations.

BELFRY -- Upper stage of a tower which houses bells.

BELLCOTES or **BELL TURRETS** -- A framework or open structure on a roof to hang bells from - usually gabled.

BEQUEST BOARDS -- A board on which a charity or bequest is recorded on the wall of a church.

BOSS -- A projecting knob or round ornament, uaually carved, covering the intersections of the ribs in a panelled ceiling or roof - or placed at the apex of a vault.

BOX PEW -- A pew with a high wooden enclosure: enclosed seating with either "high" or "low" sides.

BUTTRESS -- A mass of masonry or brick-work built against a wall to give additional strength (like at Sandon).

CADAVER TOMB -- A tomb exhibiting a sculpture of a skeleton (see Salisbury Chapel at Hatfield).

CANOPY -- A projection or hood over a door, window, etc., and the covering above a tomb or a niche. Also over a pulpit but then usually called a **TESTER**.

CAPITAL -- The top or cap of a pillar or column from which an arch springs: many capitals are ornately carved with figures or with floral designs.

CARTOUCHE -- Wall tablets within an ornate frame - usually enclosing an inscription.

CHANCEL -- That part of a church in which the altar and the choir are placed.

CHANCEL ARCH -- An arch separating the chancel from the Nave.

CHANCEL SCREEN or ROOD SCREEN -- Used to isolate the priests in the chancel from "the people" in the nave. It was also useful to keep dogs out of the chancel!

CHANTRY CHAPEL -- A small chapel usually occupying part of a larger building, espescially dedicated and endowed for chanting memorial masses for the soul of the founder or some other individual.

CHAPTER HOUSE -- The place set aside for business meetings in a Cathedral.

CHARNEL HOUSE -- A crypt or cellar in which bones removed from churchyards have been placed.

CHEVET -- A French term for the East end of a church - embracing the chancel, ambulatory and any radiating chapels.

CHEVRON -- A repetitive Norman "V" shaped design or moulding forming a zigzag.

CLERESTORY -- Uppermost storey of a church - above the nave aisle roof - which is pierced by windows. The original height of some low medieval churches was raised by building up the walls of the nave and then adding the windows to give more light.

COMMANDMENT BOARD -- Boards, often on either side of the altar, on which The Ten Commandments are written out in full.

CORBEL -- A projecting stone or piece of timber supporting a beam or vaulting on its top surface: many of these are highly ornamented with human faces - often very comical - or animals.

CORBEL TABLE -- This phrase is generally applied when corbels are used externally - particularly when a row of corbels is supporting a sloping projecting roof which may be to throw rain clear of the walls.

CREDENCE -- A shelf or table - often a slab of wood or stone inserted into the piscina recess - on which the vessels for Mass were placed before consecration.

CROCKET, CROCKETED -- Carved projections of stone in the form of leaves or flowers used to enrich spires, canopies etc., as with the stoup at Caldecote.

CROSSING -- The area where the north-south transept crosses the main chancel-nave axis of a cruciform church.

CRUCIFORM -- Usually used in the description of a church - in the shape of a right-angled cross.

CRYPT -- A chamber beneath a church and usually beneath the chancel - partly or entirely under ground.

CUPOLA -- a small rounded or polygonal domed turret crowning a roof.

DADO -- The decorative covering of the lower part of a wall.

DIAPER WORK -- Decoration of surfaces with squares, diamonds and other patterns.

DOG-TOOTH DECORATION -- Mainly Early English (13th century) decoration, consisting of four-cornered stars, found around piscinae, arches and windows.

DOOM PAINTING -- A painting depicting what might happen to evil-doers at the Last Judgement.

EASTER SEPULCHRE -- A recess provided on the north side of the chancel for the representation of the Burial and Resurrection of Christ - Used in the Middle Ages for reserving the conscrated Host between Maundy Thursday and Easter Day.

FAN VAULTING -- A number of ribs all springing from the same support and resembling an open fan.

FERETORY -- A place or chamber behind the altar where the chief shrine of a church or Cathedral is situated - particularly when watched over by a "Feretrar" - as at St.Albans.

FINIAL -- A formal bunch of foliage or similar ornament at the top of a canopy, gable or pinnacle.

FLECHE -- A slender spirelet shaped like an arrow on the roof of a church - purely for decoration.

FOLIATED -- Carved with leaf shapes.

GALILEE -- A chapel or vestibule at the western entrance of a church or Cathedral.

GARGOYLE -- Rainwater spouts projecting from church towers or wall parapets - often carved in the form of dragons or grotesque demons.

HAGIOSCOPE -- An aperture cut in a wall or pier to allow a view of the altar from places whence it could not otherwise be seen.

HAMMERBEAM -- A projecting bracket which supports the main structure of a wooden roof.

HATCHMENT -- A display of a coat of arms in a lozenge-shaped frame.

JESSE -- The name of the father of David - thus Christ's family tree: used in some churches as a decoration for a screen or window (as at Barkway).

LADY CHAPEL -- A chapel dedicated in honour of the Virgin Mary Usually at the east end of a church or Cathedral behind the high altar.

LANCET -- A long narrow window with a pointed head, typical of the 13th century.

LECTERN -- A stand to support the church Bible - it may take the form of a desk but often is an eagle with outstretched wings.

LONG AND SHORT WORK -- Saxon quoins (the dressed stones at the corners of a building) consisting of stones placed with the long sides laid alternately upright and horizontal.

LOZENGE -- A diamond-shaped pattern.

LYCH-GATE or LICH-GATE -- A covered gateway at the entrance to a churchyard: it used to be the custom for part of the burial service to be read there.

MASS DIAL -- A form of sundial used to mark the times of services by checking the position of the shadow of a central rod falling on lines in the stonework: the hour for Mass was marked with a deeper groove.

MERLON -- The solid part of an embattled parapet between the embrasures.

MISERICORD or MISERERE -- A projecting bracket - usually with amusing or grotesque figures - affixed to the underside of a seat of a choir stall so that, when the hinged seat is turned up against the back, the bracket forms a rest for the user.

NAVE -- The part of the church west of the chancel arch - where the congregation sits.

NEWEL -- The central post in a circular or winding staircase.

NICHE -- A recess in a wall for a statue, vase or other ornament.

OGEE -- A decorative arch formed by a compound curve of two parts - one convex and the other concave: sometimes seen over a piscina.

ORIEL WINDOW -- A projecting bay-window carried upon corbels or brackets.

PARCLOSE SCREEN -- A screen, of wood or stone, separating a chapel or a shrine from the rest of the church.

PARVIS or PARVISE -- Originally the term was used to refer to an area outside the west end of a church: today, however, it is generally used to describe the room over a porch.

PISCINA -- A basin with a drain at the bottom, set in a niche or recess in the wall just south of the altar, for washing the Communion or Mass vessels.

POPPY HEAD or POPPYHEAD -- The term used to describe the

decorated tops of some bench ends - derived from the French "poupee" - a puppet or figurehead.

PYX -- A vessel is which the consecrated bread is kept.

REREDOS -- An ornamental screen of wood or stone behind and above the altar.

ROOD -- The Saxon word for a Cross or Crucifix.

ROOD LOFT or ROOD BEAM -- In the 15th century, a narrow gallery was set up to carry the Rood and its images and candlesticks.

ROOD SCREEN -- The open screen below the Rood Loft spanning the east end of the nave and thus shutting off the chancel.

ROOD STAIRS -- Staircases built into the thickness of a wall near the chancel arch which used to give access to the Rood Loft.

SANCTUARY -- The area in which stands the high altar of a church.

SEDILIA -- A set of stone seats recessed into the south wall of the chancel for the use of the clergy: sometimes the sedilia and a piscina form a group together.

SLYPE -- A passageway in a Cathedral leading from the cloisters to the Cathedral - but at St.Albans between the south transept and the Chapter House.

SPANDREL -- A triangular-shaped space between the top or curve of an arch and the framwork of the doorway.

SQUINT -- An aperture cut in a wall or pier to allow a view of the altar from places whence it could not otherwise be seen.

STOUP -- Recessed basin, placed in the porch or just inside the churchdoor, containing consecrated or "holy" water.

TESTER or SOUNDING-BOARD -- A horizontal board or canopy over a pulpit to help carry the preacher's voice to the far end of the church - very necessary when three-decker pulpits were the vogue.

THREE-DECKER PULPIT -- There were three levels - the pulpit itself was situated at the top, the next level was for the reader of the Scriptures and, at the lowest or pew level, was the clerk who read the responses.

TRANSEPT -- The transverse arm of a cruciform or cross-shaped church.

TRIFORIUM -- The middle stage between the nave, or the nave arcade if there is one, and the clerestory.

TYMPANUM -- A panel, or just the space, between the lintel of a door and the arch above - and these are often filled with a design or carving.

VICE -- A winding stairway: another name for a stair turret against the outside of a church tower.

WEEPERS -- Round the sides of some tombs there may be effigies of the children, or other relatives, of the deceased: when it is the children they are often depicted in their size and age - these are known as "weepers".

ARCHITECTURAL STYLE PERIODS
OR DIVISIONS

The age of a church cannot always be estimated because one has a knowledge of historic styles, but, generally the style of architecture will convey, within fifty years or so, the date of any part of a church. The successive phases are divided into fairly well marked periods, allowing for transition between the periods: there is much overlapping because it sometimes took years for the new ideas to reach isolated places.

SAXON	7th century to 1060
NORMAN and Transition	1060 to 1190
EARLY ENGLISH and Transition	1190 to 1300
DECORATED and Transition	1300 to 1375
PERPENDICULAR and Transition	1375 to 1540

THE GAZETTEER

This alphabetical Gazetteer of religious establishments of all denominations, Christian and otherwise, is as complete as it has been possible to compile at the time of writing: any omissions are regretted and the author will be glad to know of any so that the matter can be put right should there be a revised or a second edition. The denomination of the establishment, the date, or at least the century, when the building was built, have been given, where possible, together with some details, to a lesser or greater degree, adding to those already mentioned in the historical chapters earlier.

KEY

C.of E.	Anglican - Church of England
R.C.	Roman Catholic.
L.C.	Liberal Catholic.
Bap.	Baptist
Con.	Congregational
Elim.	Elim Pentecostal Church
Meth.	Methodist
Qu.	Religious Society of Friends.
U.R.	United Reformed Church.

Any not listed above are shown individually.

ABBOTS LANGLEY

St.Lawrence, High Street. C.of E. The oldest parts are the remains of 12th century Norman nave arcades with a 13th century tower: the roof, clerestory and the tower buttresses are of the 15th century. Corbels from which the roof rafters spring are carved to represent friars in various grotesque attitudes and there are medieval wall paintings (uncovered in 1935) on each side of the east window of the Corpus Christi Chapel: one is of St.Lawrence, who was martyred by being roasted alive, holding a grid-iron. On the south aisle wall is a plaque commemorating Nicholas Breakspeare who was born at Bedmond and became, as Adrian IV, the only English Pope between 1154 and his death in 1159. The decorated font is of circa 1400 and near is a Table of Commandments. Lych-gate from High Street.
St.Saviour, The Crescent. R.C. 1963 Built of Red brick - it has a curved baptistery to one side and projecting side chapels. There is a sculpture over the entrance. Right next door is a Roman Catholic College named after Nicholas Breakspeare.
Abbots Langley Baptist Church, School Mead.
Abbots Langley Methodist Church, Langley Road.
The Church of the Ascension, Bedmond. C of E.
Bethesda Chapel, Bedmond. 1859

ALBURY

St.Mary the Virgin. C.of E. It dates back to the 13th century but has a 15th century tower with a low stair turret and a spike. Brasses on the nave floor and the south wall, and there is a tomb chest at the north end of the north aisle on which are the (unnamed) defaced effigies of a Knight and his Lady of circa 1400. Nearby is an old, padlocked oak chest.
14th century piscina in chancel, a stoup in the south aisle and there is 17th century panelling on the pulpit together with a Communion Table of the same period.

ALDBURY

St.John the Baptist. C.of E. Some 13th century remains but basically 14th century: the tower, without battlements or spike, and the two-storeyed south porch - both of late 14th century - were restored in 1905. Stone screen separates 15th century Pendley Chapel in south aisle from nave: effigies of Sir Robert Whittingham and his wife on altar tomb in chapel - his feet rest on the "Wild Man". 16th century wooden lectern and a piscina adjoining sedilia of circa 1400 in north chapel.

42 17th Century Jacobean pulpit, All Saints, Kings Langley

43 Cockerel carving on Jacobean pulpit, All Saints, Kings Langley

44 Tomb of Edmund of Langley, All Saints Church, Kings Langley

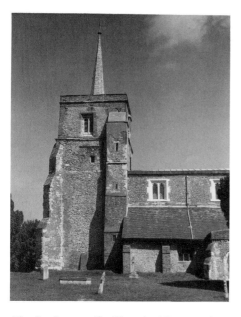

45 St. Leonard's Church, Flamstead

46 Saunders memorial, St. Leonard's Church, Flamstead

47 Praying children on the Saunders memorial, St. Leonard's Church, Flamstead

48 "Three-decker" pulpit (+ tester), St Cecilia's, Little Hadham

49 Three-decker pulpit and box pews, St. Cecilia's Church, Little Hadham

50 Jacobean pulpit, St. Michael's Church, St. Albans

51 Three-decker pulpit, St. James Church, Stanstead Abbots

52 Hour glass on pulpit, St. Michael's Church, St. Albans

53 Copper Beacon on tower, St. Mary's Church, Monken Hadley

54 The former St. Botolph's Church, now a residence, Shenley

55 St. Augustine's Church, Broxbourne   56 St James Church, Bushey

57 St. Nicholas Church, Harpenden   58 St. Etheldreda's Church, Hatfield

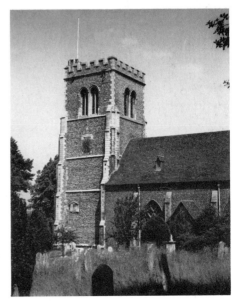

59   St. Mary's Church and Church Centre, Watford

60 Ruins of St. Etheldreda's Church, Chesfield

61 St. Etheldreda's sculpture, Chesfield

62 St. Mary Magdalene Church, Caldecote (now redundant)

63 St. Mary's Church, Kings Walden   64 All Saint's Church, Kings Langley

65 Oxhey Chapel, Oxhey

66 All Saints Church, St. Paul's Walden   67 St Giles Church, Codicote

68 "Bedhead" graveboard, St Giles Church, Codicote

69   R.C. Chapel of St. Edmund's College near Puckeridge – by Augustus Pugin

70   St. John the Evangelist, Lemsford

71 Benchend by Joseph Mayer of
Oberammergau, St. Mary's Church,
Hertingfordbury

72 St. Martin's Church, Knebworth

73 "New" Ayot St. Lawrence Church (Revett 1778-9), Ayot St. Lawrence

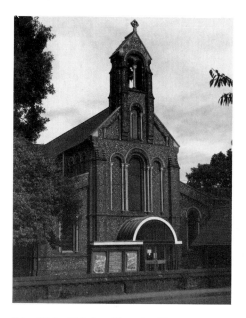
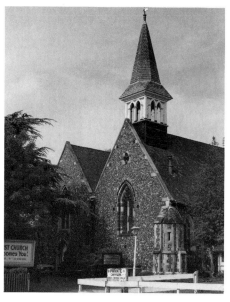

74 Holy Trinity Church, Frogmore (by Gilbert Scott 1842)

75 Christ Church, Barnet (by Gilbert Scott 1845)

76 St. Mary Magdalene Church, Flaunden (Sir Gilbert Scott's first church design)

77 Rood and Rood beam, Holy Rood Roman Catholic Church, Watford

78 Sculpture over entrance, St. Saviour's Roman Catholic Church, Abbots Langley

79 Friends meeting house, Hitchin

80 Church of Seventh-Day Adventists, St Albans

81 St. George's Church, Stevenage

82 The Jamia Mosque, Watford

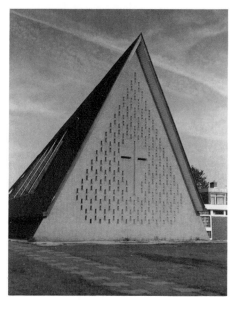

83　St. John's Church, Hilltop, Hatfield　　84　St. Andrew's Church, Cuffley

85　St. Teresa's Roman Catholic Church,　86　St. Bartholemew the Apostle R.C.
　　Boreham Wood　　　　　　　　　　　Church, St. Albans

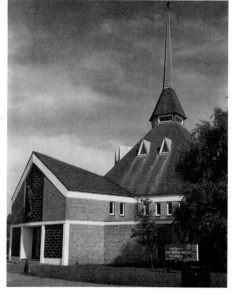

Aldbury Baptist Chapel, behind Lace Cottage, Stocks Rd. Bap.

ALDENHAM
St.John the Baptist. C.of E. Some early 13th century remains including lower part of tower but mainly building is of 14th or 15th centuries including top parts of tower: this has a stair turret higher than the embattlemented top and a thin spire - not a spike. 13th century Purbeck marble font and the remains of two piscinae and a 14th century chest nearly 10 feet long - one of the best parish coffers in England. 17th century Communion Table is in the Lady Chapel or south chapel - here also two exactly similar 14th century canopied tomb chests with effigies of ladies of the Crowmer family.

ANSTEY
St.George. C.of E. The tower is mostly Norman 12th century with a top stage of the 14th century, embattled and with a spike. The transepts - with squints to the chancel - are 13th century and, although the chancel is of the same date, the stalls - including seven misericords - are 16th century. In the chancel also is an unusual piscina and sedilia arrangement combined with a window and doorway - also graffiti. Two old chests, a Communion Table of 1637 and a crude Norman font showing four mermen holding their tails are treasures here. In churchyard is a 15th century lych-gate which had one-third bricked up as a lock-up in 1831.

ARDELEY
St.Lawrence. C.of E. Building history between early 13th century and 15th century when embattled tower was completed - spike probably added later although the present one is only of early this century. There is a piscina and a tomb recess (which may have been used as an Easter Sepulchre) both with dog-tooth decoration, and a 14th century octagonal font, but the chief glory is the 15th century roof of the nave supported by a dozen carved wooden angels all playing musical instruments. A modern rood and rood loft - but no screen - was given to the church in 1928 and there is a comparatively modern lych-gate into the churchyard.

ASHWELL
St.Mary the Virgin. C.of E. Mainly 14th century although the porches (the south being two-storeyed) are 15th: the tower, begun in the early 14th century, is 176 feet high and on the north wall of its base are the graffiti described earlier.

There are four piscinae but the main one, in the chancel, is in conjunction with a triple sedilia of circa 1380. There is a 15th century screen in the aisle but a pulpit (dated 1627) and Communion Table of the 17th century are some of the other fittings. The lych-gate is considered to be of the 15th century.

ASPENDEN
St.Mary. C.of E. Nave and chancel are late 11th century but south chancel chapel is 15th and remodelled in 1622: here are various tomb chests and recesses. The south porch, built in 1525 with small open windows now has the spaces fitted with stained glass of the four evangelists (two on each side) by Morris and Co: perhaps the last Pre-Raphaelite glass. The embattled tower is of late 14th century with a spike of 1721.

ASTON
St.Mary. C.of E A double piscina of circa 1230 in chancel gives clue to 13th century beginnings but church is mainly late 14th or early 15th century with additions in the 19th century. A screen of circa 1500 survives and there is a Communion Table together with an octagonal pulpit, both of the 17th century.

AYOT ST.LAWRENCE
Old St.Lawrence This church is now too dangerous to visit but can be viewed from the road and from where it can be seen purely as a picturesque ruin. Note the wrought iron gate.
New St.Lawrence. C.of E. 1778-9 designed by Nicholas Revett who later designed St.Pancras Church in London. Partly built as an eye-catcher - with its 4-columned porch and pavilions at the east end facing Ayot House - the altar is at west end, the reverse of what is customary.

AYOT ST.PETER
St.Peter. C.of E. 1874-5 Replacing a church destroyed by fire in 1874, the new church has an elegant broach spire which is most untypical of the county and a fancifully designed clock face. Another modern apse here with an unusual chancel arch and an iron chancel screen, reflecting - as Pevsner puts it - "Arts and Crafts tendencies."

BALDOCK
St.Mary the Virgin. C.of E. Mainly 14th century, but a double

piscina in chancel is of 13th century: in the south chapel, completed in the 15th century, is another piscina forming a group with a two-seated sedilia. A 13th century font, a Communion Table of the 17th century and two chests are some of the treasures but the 15th century screens, across both aisles and chancel arch, are the chief glories. The church was restored in 19th century but the embattled tower, with its unusual octagonal lantern between parapet and spike, remains the same as when it was built in 14th century.

Holy Trinity and St.Augustine, London Road. R.C. 1977
United Reformed Church, Whitehorse Street. U.R
Baldock Methodist Church. Meth. 1853.

BARKWAY
St.Mary Magdalene. C.of E. Earliest part 13th century but much of remainder 15th century: tower rebuilt during extensive restorations in 1861 when pinnacles were added. The nave and the aisle roofs have "vigorous" corbels and remains of a 15th century "Jesse" window are at east end of the south aisle. A 13th piscina is in chancel and a mass-dial outside.

BARLEY
St.Margaret of Antioch. C.of E. The tower is of 12th century but most of the church was rebuilt by Butterfield 1871-2 but he used much of the old material. A mutilated 15th century piscina is in south aisle but a fine Jacobean pulpit with a tester (dated 1626) remains with parts of a 15th century screen re-used against the north wall of the chancel. Outside, the tower is embattled but has Butterfield's own version of the Hertfordshire spike.

BARNET (CHIPPING BARNET)
St.John the Baptist. C.of E. Original 15th century remains including the tower but an extra nave was added when Butterfield was commissioned to enlarge the church between 1871 and 1875: font, reredos, pulpit and stained glass all by Butterfield and others so the church is now largely Victorian. There is still a piscina of the 15th century in wall of original chancel which was demolished during the restorations. Fine recumbent effigy of Thomas Ravenscroft on altar tomb under canopy, dated 1630, undisturbed in south-east chapel.

St.Stephen. A Mission Church. C.of E. The original font of circa 1452 from St.John the Baptist now here.

Christ Church, St.Albans Road. C.of E. 1845 designed by George
Gilbert Scott when he was still virtually unknown. It is of flint with
stone dressings and it has a somewhat elaborate bell turret. A north
aisle and a porch were added in 1855.
St.Peter, Arkley C of E.   1840
Mary Immaculate and St.Gregory, Union Street. R.C. 1975.
United Reformed Church, Wood Street. U.R. c.1885

BARNET (NEW BARNET)
St.Mark, Potter's Road. C.of E. 1897-8 Pulpit from St.John the
Baptist and some seating by Butterfield.
St.James, Park Road. C.of E.
Mary Immaculate and St.Peter, Somerset Road. R.C. 1938 New
Barnet Baptist Church, Lyonsdown Road. Bap.
New Barnet Baptist Church, Bevan Park.   Bap.
Underhill Baptist Church, Elton Avenue. Bap
St.John's United Reformed Church, Somerset Road. U.R.
Friends Meeting House, 55 Leicester Road. Qu.
Barnet Synagogue, Eversleigh Road. Jewish.

BARNET (EAST BARNET)
St.Mary the Virgin, Church Hill Road.C.of E. Early Norman nave
walls but rest 19th century - the tower is of 1829 but chancel is of
1880.
East Barnet Baptist Church, East Barnet Road. Bap. 1931
Methodist Church, Brookside, Cat Hill. Meth.

BARNET (MONKEN HADLEY)
St.Mary the Virgin, Hadley Green Road. C.of E. Dated accurately
as 1494 from an inscription in tower, which is embattled and has a
stair turret (high than the parapet) on which is a rare 18th century
copper beacon.   15th century font together with two piscinae, an
iron bound chest and a large number of brasses are other treasures
here.

BAYFORD
St.Mary. C.of E. 1870-1 Built near site of old church which has
disappeared but fittings in use from it - including octagonal 15th
century font. Fleche on roof, and a lych-gate..

BENGEO
St.Leonard. C.of E. circa 1120 - virtually a rare complete Norman

church with an apse. Porch only of the 18th century but the oak door is probably 14th century still with its original hinges and handles. On the left jamb of the door is a mass dial whilst in the chancel is a piscina and an aumbry: on the wall of the chancel arch is a 13th century painting of the figure of Christ being taken down from the cross. A small Norman font with a modern base, hatchments and an 19th century bellcote (but with a bell dated 1636) add to the interest here.

Holy Trinity. C. of E. 1855 - but chancel refurnished in 1884. Originally three bells taken from the temporarily abandoned St.Leonard's were hung but, in 1882, after a new set of bells arrived, the 1636 bell was returned to St.Leonard's. Tower is topped by a spire and it has a double clock-face.

BENINGTON
St.Peter. C.of E. Late 13th century or early 14th century church but tower and its spike are of 15th century. There are sedilia in the chancel of the 13th century although they have heads of circa 1330 - the date of the north chapel and the south porch - and a piscina of about the same date. A 14th century octagonal bowl on the font, a rood staircase, a chair of circa 1600 and a communion table of the 17th century together with a broken stoup in the porch are all to be seen. Under 14th century arch in north wall of chancel is an altar-tomb of circa 1320 carrying effigies of a knight in full armour plus his wife together with "weepers", and in a niche over entrance to south porch is a defaced St.Michael slaying a dragon..

BENTLEY HEATH
Holy Trinity. Cof E. 1865 The church, erected by the 2nd Earl of Stafford, stands outside the gates of Wrotham Park, between Barnet and Potters Bar.

BERKHAMSTED (GREAT BERKHAMSTED)
St.Peter. C.of E. Early 13th century chancel with nave built later in same century - but much altering and restoring over the centuries culminated in Butterfield's work between 1866 and 1888. Not only has it a 14th century south chapel (with a contemporary piscina) dedicated to St.Catherine but also what was the chantry chapel of St.John the Baptist: used by Berkhamsted School until the 1890s when their own chapel was built. Another piscina of 13th century is in the chancel but part was blocked off in 1960 when a new sanctuary was built west of the arch: however, the octagonal

purbeck marble font in the nave is of Butterfield's time when the original font went to All Saints. Various monuments include the 14th century chest tomb of a Constable of the Castle in the time of the Black Prince (who died in 1376) - Henry of Berkhamsted and his lady: the East window, however, is only of the 19th century and is a memorial to William Cowper, the poet and hymn writer, who was born here when his father was the Rector.

All Saints, Shrublands Road. C.of E. 1906 A font of 1662, originally in St. Peter's Church, is now in All Saints.

Sacred Heart Church Park Street. R.C. 1967

Berkhamsted Baptist Church, High Street. Bap. 1864

United Reformed Church, Chapel Street. U.R.

Friends' Meeting House, High Street. Qu. 1818

BISHOPS STORTFORD and HOCKERILL

St.Michael. C.of E. Whole building of one period - considered to be between 1390 and 1420 but the spire on the tower (with its lower stage now divided into three rooms since 1977) was only added in 1812. Church has a good guide showing it to be full of interest with the 18 choir stalls - all with misericords - in the chancel being the most unusual: piscinae in the chancel and the south aisle, a Purbeck marble font of circa 1150, a hexagonal oak pulpit recorded as having been made for £5 in 1658 and the substantial remains of a 15th century rood screen (but with a vaulted top of 1885) should all be noted. Finally, the many corbels in the aisles and the nave are worth studying carefully: they represent angels and many rustic characters, some with their tools and others with animal faces.

All Saints, Stanstead Road, Hockerill. C.of E. 1937 - Rebuilt after a fire in 1935.

Holy Trinity, South Street. C. of E. circa 1859 and enlarged in 1899.

St.Joseph and the English Martyrs, Windhill. R.C. Consecrated in 1906. There is a memorial to the founder of the church above the stoup at the entrance. The Sanctuary stalls are a memorial to the fallen of the First World War whilst the bronze Sanctuary gates are a memorial to those who fell in the Second World War. The windows of theLady Chapel contain some pre-Reformation glass from St.Michael's.

The Baptist Church, Newtown Road. Bap. Original church 1819 but present building erected 1899.

The Methodist Church, South Street. Meth. 1903

United Reformed Church, Water Lane. U.R. 1860

BOREHAM WOOD
All Saints. C.of E. 1910
Holy Cross. C.of E.
St.Michael and All Angels C.of E.
St.Teresa of the Child Jesus, Shenley Road. R.C. 1962-3 It has west external turrets with pyramidal roofs.
SS.John Fisher and Thomas More, Rossington Avenue. R.C. 1958
Boreham Wood Baptist Church, Furzehill Road. Bap. 1904
Boreham Wood United Reformed Church. U.R.
Boreham Wood and Elstree Synagogue, Croxdale Road. Jewish.

BOURNE END
St.John C.of E. 1854 Designed by George Gilbert Scott. The little flint church, set below the level of the road, is another with a modern apse: on the roof is Scott's version - here at any rate - of the spike although its shape qualifies it to earn the alternative name of a "snuffer".

BOVINGDON
St.Lawrence. C.of E. Entirely rebuilt in 1845 with the exception of the lower part of the walls of the west tower. As a result there is still a tomb-chest of circa 1400 on which there is an effigy of a knight in full armour. In the chancel there are several floor slabs of the 17th century, also some brasses of the same period.
Bovingdon and Flaunden Baptist Church. Bap. 1872

BOXMOOR see HEMEL HEMPSTEAD

BRAMFIELD
St.Andrew C.of E. Restoration in 1840, followed by further restoration in 1870, virtually destroyed all traces of antiquity although the church can trace a history back over 1000 years: Thomas a Becket (martyred in 1170) is reputed to have had his first living here. The simple plan of chancel, where there is a 14th century piscina, and nave has probably remained unaltered from early days: it is very different from Becket's time, and more so since the west tower, with its simple spire, was added during the 1840 restorations. There are two 14th century bells and a 17th century chest.

BRAUGHING
St.Mary the Virgin C.of E. Chancel is circa 1220 but the rest is

almost entirely 15th century.　The two-storeyed south porch, also
of the 15th century, is impressive and is higher than the south aisle:
it has an embattled parapet with crocketed pinnacles at each corner
whilst the west tower, also embattled, has a recessed spire and not
a spike.　There is a a sundial of 1871 on the porch and remains of
a medieval stoup in the south-east corner of it.　Elaborate standing
wall-monument to Brograve brothers of the early 17th century has
effigies of them both reclining with their heads propped up on their
elbows.

Braughing Chapel, Fleece Lane.　Independent　Perhaps early
18th century.

BREACHWOOD GREEN　see KINGS WALDEN

BRENT PELHAM
St.Mary the Virgin.　C.of E.　Mainly 14th century but the embattled
tower, with its spike, is 15th century.　During restorations of 1861
a south porch was added but there is a preserved 14th century door.
There are Commandment boards on either side of the nave and
stocks - with a whipping post - just outside the church gate but,
locally, the church is famous for a tomb recess in the north wall: this
is, legend says, the tomb of Piers Shonks who, supposedly, killed a
dragon.

BRICKENDON
Holy Cross and St.Alban.　C.of E.

BRICKET WOOD
St.Luke.　C.of E.

BROXBOURNE
St.Augustine.　C.of E.　Almost entirely of 15th century with some
additions in the next century and a south porch of 17th century.　The
embattled tower has a stair turret higher than the parapet and it
has a north chapel with a vestry as the second storey:　around the
top of the parapet to this is an inscription by the man who built it -
" Pray for the welfayr of Sir Wyllyam Say knyght wych fodyd yis
chapel in honor a ye trenete the yer of our Lord God 1522."　Bequest
boards at the base of the tower date back to 1440, there is a partially
destroyed piscina in the south chapel and two stoups - one in the
south aisle and the other in the south porch which has a plaque over
the door which reads "Arise ye dead and come to judgement."　A late

12th century font of purbeck marble, there are stairs leading to the
rood loft but otherwise the interior is notable for the monuments
including a memorial to John Macadam, the great improver of
British roads, who died in Broxbourne in 1836.
United Reformed Church, Mill Lane. U.R. 1966-9

BUCKLAND
St.Andrew. C.ofE. Mainly 14th century - some glass records a date
1348 - but the tower is circa 1400 and the south porch late 15th
century. A 14th century font of Barnack stone, a piscina in the
south-east corner of the south aisle, a stoup in the north wall of nave
- together with the 14th century glass fragments - are the treasures
to be found here.

BUNTINGFORD
St.Peter. C.ofE. 1614-26 : a porch and an apse were added in 1899.
Inside is a picture drawn on brass showing how the church looked
soon after it was built to attract the townspeople who found that it
was too far to walk to worship at the old church at Layston.
St.Richard of Chichester, Station Road. R.C. 1915 but consecrated
1940. The church is flint-faced with a spike.
United Reformed Church, Baldock Lane. U.R. 1819

BUSHEY
St.James, High Street. C.of E. The oldest part, the chancel, is of
the 13th century but the nave and the embattled tower, which has
a turret staircase terminating higher than the parapet, are 15th
century. Much restoration in 1871 when aisles and a north porch
were added: retained, however, were the octagonal Jacobean pulpit
with its tester and Queen Anne's coat of arms on a big 15th century
beam - in place instead of a chancel arch. There is a hatchment of
Vice-Admiral Sir Thomas Thompson who fought with Nelson at the
battles of the Nile and Copenhagen, whilst in the churchyard lies
buried Sir Hubert von Herkomer, who not only founded an Art
School but was also a pioneer in films in 1914.
The Sacred Heart of Jesus and St.John the Evangelist, London
Road. R.C. 1958-9 but consecrated 1977.
Methodist Church, London Road. Meth. 1904
Bushey Baptist Church, Chalk Hill. Bap. 1870
Bushey North Baptist Church, Park Avenue. Bap. 1955
Congregational Church, High Street. Con. 1904
Bushey Synagogue, 177-189 Sparrows Herne. Jewish.

BUSHEY HEATH
St.Peter C.of E. The chancel was built in 1891 but the rest in 1911 when the tower was also added - now a prominent landmark. The apsed St.George's Chapel was added in 1921.
Methodist Church, High Road. Meth.

BYGRAVE
St.Margaret of Antioch. C.of E. Simple church of nave and chancel only - nave of 12th century whilst chancel was rebuilt in late 14th century: in the 15th century a staircase to the rood loft was built and a small turret added to the west end to give access to the bells. There is a Communion Table and altar rails of the 17th century, 15th century octagonal font carved with the heraldry of the Passion, a 14th century piscina in the chancel, a rood screen still in situ, some 15th century poppyheaded bench ends but - rarest of all - a 17th century wrought iron hourglass stand attached to the pulpit.

CALDECOTE
St.Mary Magdalene   All of the 15th century but now declared redundant - it was closed officially in 1978. Renowned for its stoup in the porch because of its crocketed canopy.

CHESFIELD
St.Etheldreda   Down a lane between Graveley and north-east Stevenage. Built circa 1360 but is now a ruin after a licence was granted for its demolition by the Bishop of Lincoln in 1750. A modern piece of sculpture has been erected at the site to the memory of St.Etheldreda.

CHESHUNT
St.Mary the Virgin, Churchgate. C.of E. Although there are records of Vicars and Rectors going back to 1329, the present church was entirely rebuilt between 1418 and 1448 - as recorded on a brass in the chancel. The embattled tower has a stair turret higher than the parapet and this is surmounted by an 18th century cupola: this cupola, until 1912, held the bell upon which the hours had struck for 140 years. A 15th century sedilia in the chancel (now freestanding after the south chapel was built in 1872) is near the remains of a piscina of the same date which is now used as a credence. There is another piscina in the south chapel as well as an iron bound chest - probably of late 16th century - for the collection of alms. Note the corbels which support the roof - they are all carved angels carrying

shields - the 12th century font bowl and outside a medieval stone coffin (with a niche for the head) which was dug up during the building of the south chapel in 1872.
<u>United Reformed Church</u>, High Street. U.R.

CHILDWICK GREEN
<u>St.Mary</u>. C.of E. 1867 - one of the last churches designed by George Gilbert Scott. The font has two angels holding scallop shells in memoriam. Single bell in a bellcote.

CHIPPERFIELD
<u>St.Paul</u>. C.of E. 1837
<u>Our Lady, Mother of the Saviour</u>, Dunny Lane. R.C. 1989
<u>Chipperfield Baptist Church</u>, The Street. Bap. 1820

CHORLEYWOOD
<u>Christ Church</u>. C.of E. 1869-70 Built of flint and stone with a shingled spire of 1881-2 added to the tower. There is a reredos and a pulpit, both of stone, by the architect of the church, G.E.Street., and a lych-gate.
<u>St.Andrew</u>, Quickley Lane. C.of E.
<u>St.John Fisher</u>, Shire Lane. R.C. 1955
<u>Chorleywood Free Church</u>, Hillside Road. Bap. 1907
<u>Friends Meeting House</u> at Community Arts Centre, Chorleywood Common. Qu.

CLOTHALL
<u>St.Mary the Virgin</u>. C.of E. The nave, considered to be the earliest part, is of 12th century with much of remainder of 14th century. The ground stage of the tower, which has two pre-Reformation bells hung in it, forms the south porch. The wooden door, with its long iron hinges, is original and do not miss the name "John Warrin" facing into the church - probably the craftsman who made it in the 14th century. A piscina of circa 1350 is in the chapel but there is another in the chancel: whilst in the chancel look up at the east window and it will be seen to be filled with a variety of birds above the heads of Christ and St.Mary Magdalene - a gem of the 14th and 15th centuries. A 12th century font of Purbeck marble with its 17th century cover, some 15th century poppy-head bench ends and some low box pews should also be noted.

CODICOTE
St.Giles. C.of E. Early history cannot be traced with certainty because church was completely restored in 1853, but vestiges of 13th and 14th century work remain and the upper stages of the embattled tower (with spike) are 15th century. Another sign of possible antiquity is some 12th century iron scroll work and there is a Jacobean pulpit. Outside do not miss the bedhead graveboard near the lych-gate.

COLNEY HEATH
St.Mark. C.of E. 1845 Another comparatively modern apsed east end to the church, and there is a small gallery inside.

COTTERED
St.John the Baptist. C.of E. Mainly 14th century with an embattled tower of the same period and a somewhat larger than usual spike. The north (now blocked) and south doorways are also of the same period but the south door is 15th century. Sedilia and piscina in the chancel are of the 14th century whilst there are two other piscinae elsewhere: there is a font of 1739 made of grey Derbyshire marble but the chief treasure is a large wall painting of St.Christopher on the north wall of the aisleless nave. There are windmills in the wall painting but there is also a graffito of a postmill elsewhere in the church.

CROXLEY GREEN
All Saints C.of E. 1870-2 but in 1907 a new nave was added to the south of the old one. The church has an unusual round tower.
St.Oswald, Malvern Way. C.of E.
St.Bede, Baldwins Lane. R.C. Consecrated 1975
Croxley Green Baptist Church, Baldwins Lane. Bap. 1942
Croxley Green Methodist Church, New Road. Meth.

CUFFLEY
St.Andrew. C.of E. 1965 The church physically dominates the village by being on an elevated site. It has a steeply pitched roof on very visible concrete supports.
Cuffley Free Church. Bap. 1965-7 It has a central spirelet.

DATCHWORTH
All Saints. C.of E. Nave is of 12th century but other parts range from then to 16th century with a tower of the 14th century but with

a 19th century broach spire which was added during restorations in 1875. There is an octagonal font of the 15th century and also in the nave, a recess containing a stone slab with a floriated cross on it whilst in the chancel is a chair of the 17th century. Outside note the coffin covers and bedhead graveboards in the churchyard.
Wesleyan Church, Burnham Green. Originally built as a school in 1841.

DIGSWELL see WELWYN GARDEN CITY.

EASTWICK
St.Botolph. C.of E. Church rebuilt in 1872 when the 13th century chancel arch was rebuilt using the original materials - richly moulded and the arch rests on detached shafts of Purbeck marble and is, as Pevsner says, " an astonishingly ambitious piece of 13th century design." Reputedly the oldest effigy in the county is the marble figure of a knight, in complete chain mail and long surcoat, together with a long shield - mid 13th century and in the tower. The embattled tower itself retained its gargoyles when it was partly rebuilt in 1873. Note that this is now the only church dedicated to St.Botolph in the county (see Shenley).

ELSTREE
St.Nicholas. High Street. C.of E. Largely a creation of 1853 although some of the material of the old 15th century building was re-used: the nave was rebuilt on the old foundations using columns and capitals of the old south arcade etc. The octagonal font is of the 15th century but it has a modern cover of 1974. A 1603 alabaster monument to Olive Buck was repaired and replaced on the north wall early this century.

ESSENDON
St.Mary the Virgin. C.of E. Entirely rebuilt in 1883 except for the west tower which is of the 15th century but much restored - it is embattled and has a spike on which is a decorative wind-vane. Church was bombed in a Zeppelin raid in 1916 with damage to the chancel, organ and many windows but the Black Basalt ware Wedgewood font, presented to the church in 1778 by Mary Whitbread, was undamaged. It is a very precious relic, the only other similar one is at Cardington, the home of the Whitbreads, in Bedfordshire, so you will have to ask to see it: normally a run-of-the-mill Victorian font is used for christenings. Note also the commandment boards

on the south wall and opposite a panel showing the Royal Arms which is actually a piece of weaving - also by Mary Whitbread.

FLAMSTEAD
St.Leonard. C.of E. Most of the church is of the 13th century with the chancel re-modelled in the 14th century but the west tower is circa 1120: the top stage, without battlements, was added when the clerestory was formed in the 15th century and this supports a rebuilt spike of 1974. There is a piscina with sedilia in the chancel, another piscina in the south chapel, a 17th century Communion Table and a 15th century font but the chief glories here are the wall paintings which are, according to Pevsner, " Apart from St.Albans, the most important series in the county." Note also the Saunders memorial, the 15th century screen with its 1912 rood carved in Oberammergau and the Sebright family connections including hatchments: in the churchyard the chest tomb of Thomas Pickford, the founder of the haulage firm.

FLAUNDEN
St.Mary Magadalene. C.of E. 1838 George Gilbert Scott's first church although he called it " the poor barn designed for my uncle." The old church, mentioned earlier in chapter 6, is now just a few stones but Scott's church obtained from it a 15th century font, some worn medieval tiles in the porch and three bells - one dated 1578 - in the little bellcote at the west end.

FROGMORE
Holy Trinity C.of E. 1842 Another early church designed by George Gilbert Scot in a neo-Norman style. Accordingly, it has an apse at the east end and a rather large bellcote over the west end.

FURNEUX PELHAM
St.Mary the Virgin. C.of E. The chancel is dated circa 1260-80 but the embattled tower with its spike and gargoyles was added later in circa 1370: note the detail surrounding the clock below a window of the bell chamber. Possibly of the 17th century, a figure of Father Time surmounts the clock, proclaiming that "Time Flies" and "Mind Your Business". The south porch, also embattled, has two storeys but it was rebuilt during 1869 restorations: at the same time the south chapel gained some memorial windows by the Pre-Raphaelite craftsmen, William Morris and Burne-Jones. Inside also are 13th century three-fold sedilia with a piscina - together with an Easter

Sepulchre - in the chancel, another piscina of the 16th century in the south chapel, some tomb chests and the remains of a stoup in the porch.

GARSTON see WATFORD

GILSTON
St.Mary C.of E. Basically 13th century built of flint with stone dressings but the tower is of brick: it was re-constructed late in the 16th century and is now embattled with a spike. The chief nterest here is the remains of a 13th century screen because it is an unusually early example of woodwork. The bowl of the font is even older - of the 12th century - and in the north aisle there is a late 13th century coffin lid with a floriated cross cut in relief. A combined piscina and credence are in the chancel together with 17th century memorials of various kinds to the Gore family.

GOFFS OAK
St.James. C.of E. 1860 A little church of yellow brick with a somewhat unusual bell turret topped by a spire. The pulpit was originally in St.Mary's Church, Cheshunt and it has an oak eagle lectern.
Methodist Church, Ordnance Road. Meth.

GRAVELEY
St.Mary. C.of E. The nave is probably 12th century and the chancel with its double piscina is 13th century: the embattled tower, with a spike in the form of a cross, is dated circa 1480 but the south porch is 18th century. There is another piscina in the nave and the remains of a 15th century rood screen of traceried oak. There are graffiti to be found on the door jamb and on the south jamb of the tower arch and, finally, note the "bedhead" graveboard and the grave cover in the churchyard.

GREAT AMWELL
St.John the Baptist. C.of E. The church, with its Norman apse - one of only three in the county - is dated late 11th century although the embattled tower, with its more modern pyramidal spire, is 15th century along with the west door. On each side of the 11th century chancel arch is a round-headed squint inserted at an unknown later date. A piscina and sedilia in the chancel, another 14th century

piscina in the south wall of the nave, a Communion Table and a pulpit of the early 17th century are to be found, but otherwise there is a lot of interest in the churchyard with its variety of monuments and old stocks.

GREAT GADDESDEN

St.John the Baptist. C.of E. The east wall of the chancel is 12th century but it has Roman bricks in its buttresses and some of the corner stones: the chancel and the nave are probably of that date but the clerestory and the west tower are of the 15th century. There are grotesque gargoyles on the tower with its embattled parapet and high stair turret: they are, no doubt, contemporary with its building, but, inside, the angels on the roof corbels were only put up between 1912 and 1914. There is a piscina in the chancel as well as Commandment boards on either side of the altar, and elsewhere two Communion Tables and two chests - one cut from a log. The north chapel, built in 1730 as a memorial chapel to the Halsey family, contains over 20 such memorials to members of that family. In the churchyard there are a number of tomb chests below the east window and under the east window is a stone with "IHS" cut into it.

GREAT HORMEAD

St.Nicholas. C.of E. Much restored in 1874, the church dates back to circa 1300 with the top stage of the embattled tower being built in the 15th century at the same time as the clerestory. There are gargoyles outside and there are "grotesque" corbels inside and a Norman font of the late 12th century is still in situ.

GREAT MUNDEN

St.Nicholas. C.of E. The chancel arch is of circa 1120 along with the nave and the chancel itself but the south aisle is of circa 1350: here are two ogee-headed tomb recesses and an early 15th century stone reredos which was, for years, hidden behind plaster. A Jacobean pulpit and some 16th century stalls with the initials "R.K." carved on some of them are also to be seen inside whilst outside the embattled 15th century tower has a spike and gargoyles at the angles.

GREAT WYMONDLEY

St.Mary the Virgin. C.of E. The third of the three Norman apse churches, with the chancel and nave both being 12th century Norman with windows inserted over the next three centuries: the

embattled tower is 15th century with a pyramidal roof. The nave
roof is of the same period and supported by a number of corbels - a
king, a nun, a shaggy lion etc. A squint on one side of the chancel
arch looks on to the altar, and in the chancel is a double piscina.
There is a 15th century octagonal font, a few repaired benches of the
same period but note the remains of a mass dial outside on the south
wall of the nave.

HARPENDEN
St.Nicholas. C.of E. The embattled tower, with its stair turret
higher than the parapet and its spike, is of the 15th century and it
was built at the west end after a fire destroyed an earlier central
tower, but the rest of the building was entirely rebuilt in 1862: there
are, however, some capitals on window ledges from the 12th century
church. There is also a 12th century Purbeck marble font bowl (on
a 19th century base) - a rare treasure here. The weather vane on
the top of the spike is a ship in full sail - St.Nicholas is the Patron
Saint of sailors - and in the north aisle is a large White Ensign from
"HMS Harpenden", a mine-sweeper of the First World War.
St.John the Baptist, St.John's Road. C.of E. Built in 1908 to replace
a previous church which burnt down in 1905.
All Saints, Station Road. C.of E. After several years of planning,
actual building started in 1964 and this modern church was conse-
crated in 1965 by the then Bishop of St.Albans - the little Mission
Room, built originally in 1860 for the first local worshippers, having
served its purpose was demolished. The stainless steel cross, above
what could just be called a spike, is 60 feet above ground and the font
is of Cornish granite.
St.Mary, Kinsbourne Green. C.of E.
Our Lady of Lourdes, Rothamsted Avenue. R.C. Built between
1926 and 1936 when it was consecrated.
Methodist Church, High Street. Meth. 1929
Methodist Church, Kinsbourne Green. Meth
Methodist Church, South Harpenden. Meth
Methodist Church, Lower Luton Road, Batford. Meth.
United Reformed Church, Victoria Road. U.R. 1897
Friends Meeting House, Southdown Road. Qu.
Evangelical Church, Vaughan Road.
Evangelical Free Church, Crabtree Lane.

HATFIELD
St.Etheldreda, Church Street. C.of E. The chancel and the

transepts date from the 13th century as proved by the piscina and the dogtooth decoration in the south transept but the embattled tower (with no spike) was built in its present position in the 15th century when a central tower was destroyed to enable the nave to be widened. The Brocket Chapel dates from the same period but the Salisbury Chapel was built in 1618 by the 2nd Earl of Salisbury to hold the tomb of his father, Sir Robert Cecil, the 1st Earl who died in 1612 before his Hatfield House was completed. An elaborate monument indeed: the effigy of Robert Cecil lies on black marble slab, in his Garter robes, supported by the four kneeling Cardinal Virtues - but beneath the effigy lies a skeleton on a rough straw mat! There are various other memorials including those in the Brocket Chapel. A wrought-iron screen of the 18th century, originally in Amiens Cathedral, separates the Salisbury Chapel from the chancel, some Jacobean altar rails but the pulpit was designed by Sir Albert Richardson in 1947 as a War Memorial to the dead of the two World Wars.

St.Michael and All Angels, Birchwood. C.of E. 1955

St.Luke, Town Centre. C.of E. Built originally in 1877 as a cemetery chapel but enlarged in 1893 into a church.

St.John's Church, Hilltop. C.of E. 1960-2 A modern design with an unusual shape.

Marychurch, Old Hatfield R.C. Planned in 1962 but built 1969-70. The original church on the site, dedicated to The Blessed Sacrament and St.Teresa, is now the church hall.

St.Peter, Bishops Rise, Hatfield South. R.C. 1961

Birchwood Methodist Church, Birchwood. Meth.

Christ Church Congregational Church, St.Albans Road. Con.

Friends Meeting House, Wellfield Close. Qu.

HEMEL HEMPSTEAD

St.Mary, High Street. C.of E. Church begun circa 1140 and finished about 40 years later so, apart from the Cathedral, the oldest in the county. Unusually in the county, the spire (which rises to nearly 200 feet) on top of an unembattled parapet, is of the 13th century and has a circular staircase turret on the south-east side. There is a piscina of the 14th century in the chancel and one of the 15th century in the south transept contemporary with the building of it. In a church with few monuments, the monument to Sir Astley Paston Cooper -the "sergeant-surgeon" to George IV, William IV and Queen Victoria - is the most conspicuous.

St.Mary, Aspley End. C.of E. 1871 The church has a north-east tower with a spire.

St.John the Evangelist, Boxmoor. C,of E. Planned 1868-70 and built 1873-4 - designed by Norman Shaw. Church has two aisles and the nave was extended in 1893: there is a turret above the former nave end.

Holy Trinity, Leverstock Green. C.of E. 1846 A small church with a double bellcote: a rood screen, stalls and an altar of 1932.

St.Paul, Highfield. C.of E. 1869

St Barnabas, Everest Way, Adeyfield. C.of E. 1952.

St.Stephen, Chaulden. C.of E.

St.Alban, Warners End. C.of E. A church in the modern style, designed by the Development Corporation's chief architect, but nevertheless has a spike.

St.Benedict, Bennetts End. C.of E.

SS.Mary and Joseph, St.John's Road, Boxmoor. R.C.

Our Lady Queen of All Creation, St.Albans Road, Adeyfield. R.C. Consecrated 1987.

St.Paul, Highfield. R.C. 1971 (Shared)

Church of the Resurrection, Grove Hill. R.C. 1977 (Shared)

St.Peter, Gadebridge. R.C. 1977

Hemel Hampstead Baptist Church, Belmont Road. Bap. 1962

Marlowes Baptist Church, The Marlowes. Bap. 1861 replacing the original chapel erected in 1679 in Crown Yard.

Boxmoor Baptist Church, London Road. Bap. 1826 and extended in 1864.

Grove Hill Baptist Church, Grove Hill. Bap.

Methodist Church, The Marlowes. Meth.

Congregational Church, Alexandra Road. Con.

Friends Meeting House, St.Mary's Road. Qu. 1718

St.George's United Reformed Church, Long Chaulden. U.R.

Adeyfield Free United Reformed Church, Leverstock Green Road.

HERTFORD

St.Andrew, St.Andrew's Street. C.of E. Completely rebuilt in 1869 but retains the north doorway of the old 15th century church and there is a stoup of that period also. A 17th century Communion table and a brass and some slabs - all probably from the old church. The steeple, a gift of Earl Cowper, was completed in 1876: the transepts, the south as the chapel of St.Nicholas in 1947 and the north as the chapel of St.Mary in 1950, were furnished to perpetuate the old tradition that in the former church south and north aisles were added when the former parishes of St.Nicholas and St.Mary were added to St.Andrew in the 16th century.

All Saints. C.of E. Built in 1893-5 on the site of an earlier church destroyed by fire in 1891: the tower - put up in 1905 "in memory of the glorious reign of our beloved Queen Victoria" - has what Pevsner calls " an alien look" about it with its pinnacles on the parapet and is not typical of the county at all. There is a fine alabaster reredos depicting the Last Supper and a splendid memorial to the men of the Hertfordshire Regiment who fell in the two World Wars.

The Immaculate Conception and St.Joseph, St.John Street. R.C. Consecrated 1862.

Hertford Baptist Church, Port Hill. Bap. 1906-7

Congregational Church, Cowbridge. Con. 1862

Methodist Chapel, Ware Road. Meth.

Friends Meeting House, Railway Street. Qu. 1670 This is the oldest purpose-built Friends' Meeting House in the world.

HERTINGFORDBURY

St.Mary. C.of E. Much restored by Earl Cowper of Panshanger in 1891, the church in reality dates from before 1400: the alabaster font, reredos, sedilia and pulpit reflect the restoration but are surpassed by the bench ends carved in the Baroque style by Joseph Mayer of Oberammergau (invited to England by Earl Cowper) whose name is carved on the first pew. The embattled tower with its spike is of the 15th century but otherwise the monuments here, including the Cowper Chapel surrounded by iron railings erected during the restorations in 1891, must be noted. In the churchyard note the altar tomb with legs!

HEXTON

St.Faith. C.of E. Chancel and nave are 13th century although the tower, which partially collapsed in 1948, is 15th century. The 15th century roof of the nave is supported by carved corbels and half-length figures of angels supporting the intermediate rafters. Below are commandment boards, a double-decker pulpit and a reading desk.

HIGH CROSS

St.John the Evangelist. C.of E. 1846 The church has a south-east steeple. Contrasting styles of stained glass by C.E.Kempe (who is responsible for a lot of glass in the county) and Selwyn Image.

HIGH WYCH

<u>St.James</u>. C.of E. 1861 Already referred to in chapter 4 where I quoted Pevsner's remark that "it deserves to be specially mentioned as an eminently typical example of High Victorian design at its most revolting ": he also said, however, that it was " as original in its handling of Gothic forms as anything in the Art Nouveau of forty years later." It has a circular turret and a spirelet.

HINXWORTH

<u>St.Nicholas</u>. C.of E. The nave and the west tower, both embattled, are early 15th century but the little chancel of brick, looking every bit as if it was an after-thought, is 18th century, whilst the clerestory is 16th century. In the nave roof are four oak angels, the stairs of the old rood loft remain and in the 15th century south porch is a 14th century coffin lid.

HITCHIN

<u>St.Mary</u>, Churchyard Walk. C.of E. Much building history here but basically the present church dates from the 14th and 15th centuries (see guidebook), although there were earlier churches on the site. A guidebook is essential here because there is so much of interest but the chief glory is the series of screens with the angel screen to the south chapel (with its angel corbels) being considered one of the finest in the country. There are also many corbels in the nave where the 15th century font has the 12 apostles around the base although defaced during the Civil War: the pulpit is also 15th century. In the north aisle is the entrance to the unique Charnel House and in the north chapel itself is a 17th century Communion Table and a piscina plus credence on the east wall: realise at this point that there is an almost unique ambulatory behnd the high altar. There is the remains of a stoup in the north porch and a tympanum above the medieval door in the south porch - both porches are two-storeyed and the heavy embattled tower with its spike and stair turret has a sundial on it in thanksgiving for the restoration of Charles II.

<u>Holy Saviour</u>, Radcliffe Road. C.of E. 1863-5 designed by Butterfield in Early English style - a west bellcote instead of a tower. Aisles were added in 1880-3.

<u>St.Faith</u>, Woolgrove Road. C.of E.

<u>St.John</u>, St.John's Road. C.of E.

<u>St.Mark</u>, Lancaster Avenue. C.of E.

<u>**Our Lady Immaculate and St.Andrew**</u>, Nightingale Road. R.C.

consecrated 1977.

<u>Hitchin Baptist Church</u>, Tilehouse Street. Bap.   The present building, with its four Tuscan columns and pediment over all, was erected in 1844 on the site of a chapel with its connections with John Bunyan: this church can trace its formation back to 1669 and today there is a chair presented by Bunyan when he used to preach in the old chapel.

<u>Walsworth Baptist Church</u>, Walsworth Road. Bap. 1869

<u>Friends Meeting House</u>, Paynes Park. Qu. 1958-9 An L-shaped modern building which is built on stilts.

<u>Methodist Church</u>, Hampden Road. Meth.

<u>Bethel Chapel</u>, Queen Street.

HODDESDON

<u>St.Paul</u>. C.of E.   A private chapel was built in 1732 by Robert Plomer but the church did not become parochial until 1844: in 1864-6 the present church was built out of the original chapel and the 18th century gallery was retained. An uncharacteristic red brick tower with a pyramidal roof fails to dominate the tower block in the Market Place where St.Katherine's Chapel used to be situated: it was demolished in 1835 so that the present clock tower could be erected. An old print shows that it had a small embattled tower with a spike.

<u>St.Augustine</u>, High Street. R.C. 1962

<u>Hoddesdon Baptist Church</u>, Burford Street. Bap. 1911

<u>Friends Meeting House</u>, Lord Street. Qu.

HOLWELL

<u>St.Peter</u> C.of E. Completely rebuilt in 1877-79 but with the use of some of the old materials: a 15th century doorway, a piscina, much damaged, of the same period and a Communion Table at the east end of the side aisle can be found but the most interesting relic is the flagstone with three small 1515 brasses to the memory of a pre-Reformation rector, Robert Wodehouse.

HUNSDON

<u>St.Dunstan</u>. C.of E. The building was restored in the 19th century but not structurally altered, although in earlier centuries in circa 1500 the nave was widened and the chancel rebuilt. The chief point of interest here is the Jacobean screen in front of the Carey Chapel with its high family pews - probably of the same date as the pulpit with its tester. Two doors and part of the stairs to the rood loft

remain and there is a piscina in the chancel: a Communion Table and a poor box, both of the 17th century, are treasured and the wooden north porch is believed to be the oldest in the county. The embattled tower is of the 15th century and it is reputed to have the spike that was removed from the tower of the Cathedral.

HUNTON BRIDGE
St.Paul C.of E. 1865 designed by H.Woodyer who also was responsible for the stone reredos, pulpit, screen and the font. It has a very ornamental chancel arch much embellished, along with the rest of the interior, with angels. There is a tall shingled wooden broach spire on top of the tower.

ICKLEFORD
St.Katherine. C.of E. The nave is circa 1150, the chancel and the west tower were built early in the 13th century: the tower, which is entirely covered with plaster like the rest of the church, has a low pyramidal roof and a form of spike. The tower is not embattled but the south porch of circa 1450 is: the doorway itself is 12th century as is the now blocked north doorway and both have Norman zigzag arches. The nave roof of the 15th century has a variety of grotesque stone corbels which were not disturbed by Sir George Gilbert Scott's restorations in 1859. There are screen remains here, a rood loft staircase and 15th century piscina in the chancel.

IPPOLLITTS
St.Ippolyts. C.of E. Almost the whole church, except the 14th century tower, was rebuilt from the foundations in 1879 but the old materials dating from Norman times (the nave was built towards the end of the 11th century) were carefully replaced so that the building retained much of its original shape. The tower is embattled but has a pyramidal roof with a crossed spike and a 14th century piscina, complete with credence, has also been retained in the chancel: there are also piscinae of the same period in the two aisles. The south porch is of 15th century timber framing with 17th century brick sides but the roof is modern. Note that the church is one of only two in England dedicated to St. Hippolytus, an eminent bishop and theologian who lived in the 3rd century.

KELSHALL
St.Faith. C.of E. The church is mainly of the 15th century but, except for the embattled tower with its spike, was completely

restored in 1870. The south porch is two-storeyed and the door, which is original, is of oak and retains the old lock and ironwork: there is a staircase to the room over the porch which also has old ironwork. In the north aisle is a tall narrow recess measuring 12ft by 1ft 8in - possibly unique - which probably held a processional cross or stave, and in the south aisle is a damaged 15th century piscina. Outside, there is the base of an octagonal stone cross and a modern lych-gate.

KIMPTON
St.Peter and St.Paul. C.of E. Much of the church is of circa 1200 although the nave is probably earlier: the embattled tower with a spike and the two-storeyed porch, with its turret staircase, were added in the 15th century but there is one bell here which is even older dating from the mid-14th century. The later 15th century roof of the south aisle is supported by corbels carved as angels and there is a St.Christopher wall painting over the north arcade. A screen separates the chancel and south chapel where there is a 13th century piscina and, at the west end of the chapel, a restored rood screen. Note also the six poppy-headed bench ends of the 15th century.

KINGS LANGLEY
All Saints. C.of E. Mainly 15th century although the walls of the chancel are of the 13th century: the embattled tower with a spike and a stair turret to the belfry is also of the 15th century but of a later date than the nave. There is a 13th century piscina in the chancel but the pulpit and the memorials here are the chief items of interest. The most important tomb is that of Edmund of Langley, who was the 5th son of Edward III and became the very first Duke of York: the tomb, in the north aisle, is surrounded with alabaster heraldry and is similar in design to the tomb of his elder brother, The Black Prince, in Canterbury Cathedral. The early 17th century pulpit is elaborately carved and has two carved crowing cocks on it - to signify the cock crowing to St.Peter - and is surmounted by a tester. Note also the reredos, crammed with figures, put up over the altar in 1878.
R.C. The Local History Guide (1987) states that Catholic worshippers have the use of the Parish Church.
Christ Church Baptist Church, The Nap. Bap. 1938
Baptist Chapel, Waterside. Strict Bap. 1835
Methodist Church, Hempstead Road. Meth. 1935 - a new building:

the Methodists first met together locally in 1870.

KINGS WALDEN

St.Mary. C.of E. The embattled west tower, with its stair turret, is dated circa 1380 but the nave has late 12th century arcades: the clerestory, however, was added in the 15th century together with battlements on the roof. There is a 13th century double piscina in the chancel and another one in the north aisle but many of the fittings date from the time of 1868 restoration: also stained glass at this period by William Morris.

Baptist Chapel at Breachwood Green. Bap. 1904 Two dwarf turrets and a lot of ironwork are prominent at the west end of the roof. Inside there is a pulpit of 1658 - John Bunyan is reputed to have preached from it.

KNEBWORTH

St.Mary and St.Thomas. C.of E. This church, standing in the grounds of Knebworth House, has a varied building history: nave and chancel of circa 1150, north chapel of circa 1520, the south porch of circa 1600 but the embattled west tower, with its spike, gargoyles and stair turret, is dated 1420 and is perhaps the only part of the building to remain as built. The north chapel was rebuilt circa 1700 to house the Lytton monuments for which this church is particularly noted. There is a 14th century piscina in the chancel, a 14th century octagonal font, a complete set of 15th century oak benches in the nave and the pulpit, of the 18th century, has carved panels of Flemish origin and one is dated 1567. Finally, note the iron grill of 1700 under the tower arch, and the iron screen and gates to the Lytton Chapel designed by Lutyens circa 1933.

St.Martin, London Road. C.of E. 1914 by Sir Ewdwin Lutyens but completed by Sir Albert Richardson in 1963-4: it has no tower but very deep roof eaves and a simple bell cupola with a weather vane on top. A complete contrast inside to traditional churches and this design of Lutyens may well have influenced many of the designs for postwar churches after the Second World War.

St.Thomas More, London Road. R.C. 1936

Knebworth United Reformed Church, Park Lane. U.R.

LANGLEY (Between Hitchin and Langley)

Minsden Chapel. Probably of the 14th century. Ruined remains of a chancel and nave.

LAYSTON (See Buntingford)

St.Bartholemew. C.of E. Chancel of 13th century but most of the rest is 15th century with the embattled tower still with its spike. However, the church was finally closed in 1951 and the roofless building deteriorates as the years go by.

LEVERSTOCK GREEN see HEMEL HEMPSTEAD

LEMSFORD

St.John the Evangelist. C.of E. 1858-9 with a chapel added in 1930. The tower has a set of medieval-style gargoyles and a stair turret: no battlements or spike but there are battlements on the south chapel built for the Nall-Caine family.

LETCHWORTH

St.Mary the Virgin, Letchworth Lane. C.of E. The original church in the area and, with a nave probably of the 12th century, without doubt the oldest building in the Garden City. There is 13th century ironwork on the south door, the base of a stoup in the porch of the same period, the font bowl is 14th century and a pre-Reformation bell, with "Ave Maria Gracia Plena" inscribed on it, has continued to ring in the timber bell turret.

All Saints, Willian. C.of E. The chancel and the nave were built in the first half of the 12th century, but the embattled west tower with its stair turret and gargoyles (some of the best in the county) is circa 1430. The south porch is 15th century also but the most interesting part of the church is the chancel: here is a fine wall monument of 1625 to the Lacon family but the 15th century stalls, with their fine carved bench ends, have now been removed. They have not, however, disappeared completely because great ingenuity has preserved three by making them up into a large chair (for the Bishop?): an elephant, complete with howdah, and John the Baptist's head on a charger on the two ex-bench ends making up the side pieces of the chair, are extraordinary examples of the 15th century woodcarvers' art.

St.Nicholas, Norton. C.of E. The chancel was entirely rebuilt in 1814 but there are Norman remains in the nave although it was lengthened and enlarged in the 15th century when the embattled tower with its stair turret was built. The octagonal font is of the 13th century, there are stalls in the nave of circa 1500 and there is another pre-Reformation bell here inscribed "Sancte Petre ora pro nobis." There is a hexagonal Jacobean pulpit with a tester.

St.George, Norton Way North. C.of E. 1961-4 A distinctive modern church, designed by the same architect as St.John's Church in Hatfield: it has a tall concrete spire which goes through the roof to serve as a backdrop to the altar and the crucifix. The font - another modern feature - is a ring around the concrete pier which supports the west end.

St.Paul, Pixmore Way. C.of E. Begun 1923 but not completed.

St.Michael the Archangel, The Broadway. C.of E. 1966-8 It has a cupola and a spirelet with a Lady Chapel at the west end.

St.Thomas of Canterbury, Bedford Road. C.of E.

St.Hugh of Lincoln, The Broadway. R.C. Designed in 1938 but not built until 1960.

The Church of St.Alban, Meadow Way. L.C.

Baptist Church, West View. Bap.

Danescroft Baptist Church, Grange Estate. Bap.

Elim Pentecostal Church, Norton Way North. Elim. 1925

Free Church (Interdenominational), Norton Way South.

Central Methodist Church, Norton Way South. Meth.

Methodist Church, North Avenue. Meth.

Friends Meeting House, "Howgills", South View. Qu. 1907

LETTY GREEN
St.John. C.of E. 1849 - originally built as a chapel of ease for Hertingfordbury.

LILLEY
St.Peter. C.of E. A completely new church was built in 1870-1 with the original 12th century chancel arch re-set in the north wall of the present chancel, which has coloured shields depicting various symbols of St.Peter covering the ceiling. The pulpit is made of oak from the old chapel of St.John's College, Cambridge, which was also being pulled down in 1871 but the 15th century font and the re-set piscina are both from the old church.

LITTLE AMWELL
Holy Trinity. C.of E. 1863

LITTLE BERKHAMSTED
St.Andrew. C.of E. There was a church built in 1647 but nothing remains except that parts of the east and west walls are thought to have been part of it - the present building only dates from Victorian times. Bishop Thomas Ken, the writer of hymns and the

well known doxology "Praise God from whom all blessings flow", was born in the parish in 1637 and the chancel altar was given in his memory. One of the bells in the wooden bellcote is of the 14th century and there is floor slab to show that Cromwell's grandson, Cromwell Fleetwood, is buried here.

LITTLE GADDESDEN
St.Peter and St.Paul. C.of E. The early history is obscure because of restoration and rebuilding: The nave and the embattled tower of the 15th century appear to be the oldest parts but the chancel was rebuilt in the 17th century with the south porch, originally of the same period, was rebuilt by Sir Jeffry Wyattville in 1830 whilst he was engaged on the rebuilding of Ashridge. There are poppyheads on 17th century benchends and the remains of a screen between chancel and nave but otherwise, in the words of Pevsner, the church is "Architecturally less important than for its monuments" to the occupants of Ashridge - including the 3rd Duke of Bridgewater who died in 1803, the inspiration behind the Grand Union Canal.

LITTLE HADHAM
St.Cecilia. C.of E. The nave is possibly 12th century although this is uncertain: certain, however, is the fact that the embattled tower, with a spike, is 14th century and the wooden south porch has survived from the 15th century. Even rarer inside the church, but of the 17th century, is the three-decker pulpit and a tester, dated 1633, and the box pews which have all been carefully preserved. There is also a fine early 16th century rood screen and the church guide directs you to note the slab on the south side of the altar to Arthur Capel (of Hadham Hall) who was "Murdered for his loyalty to his King." (Charles I).

LITTLE HORMEAD
St.Mary. C.of E. An isolated little church but one of the oldest in the county: Nave is circa 1140 and the chancel was rebuilt in circa 1220. The octagonal font of circa 1310, a piscina in the chancel and the remains of a stoup in the porch should all be noted but the real treasure here is the 12th century ironwork on the north doorway - a rare survival. This doorway is, of course, no longer in use but the south doorway is also Norman although the the little brick porch was only added in the 18th century.

LITTLE MUNDEN

All Saints C.of E. Much restored but the church dates back to circa 1100 - in the chancel is a 12th century doorway which, according to Pevsner, proves a nave and chancel at least 800 years old: early in the 15th century the north chapel was enlarged to its present size and later in the century the embattled tower with a spike was added. In the chancel are two altar tombs with effigies in armour and their ladies - of the 14th and 15th centuries - and there is also a piscina of the 14th century. A screen of the 15th century under the west arch of the north chapel completes the antiquities.

LITTLE WYMONDLEY

St.Mary the Virgin. C.of E. The chancel, nave and west tower are probably of the second half of the 15th century but this is uncertain because the church was completely restored in 1875. There is a 15th century piscina in the chancel wall and a niche for an image of the 16th century but otherwise little of note.

LONDON COLNEY

St.Peter. C.of E. 1825 There is a west gallery here on cast-iron columns and stained glass of 1865 designed by the Dowager Marchioness of Waterford.

Our Lady of Walsingham, Haseldine Road. R.C. 1959 It has two west towers with spikes.

Chapel of the All Saints Pastoral Centre. R.C. Centre begun 1899 but the Chapel was started in 1927 and extended in 1964.

London Colney Baptist Church, Kings Road. Bap. 1938

LONG MARSTON

All Saints. C.of E. 1882 The 15th century tower in Chapel Lane is all that remains of the old 12th century which was demolished in 1883, nut the new church contains a number of details from the old one - and some from Tring. A 14th century font and a piscina of the same century - even a recess of the 13th century with dogtooth ornament - are all, together with a partly 15th century screen and a 17th century hexagonal pulpit, to be found in this late 19th century church!

Long Marston Baptist Chapel. Bap.

Long Marston Methodist Chapel. Meth.

MARKYATE
St.John the Baptist.   C.of E.   Built in 1734, the church is now
somewhat cut off from the village by the bypass but it is still the
parish church.   It has a small but embattled west tower, a carved
pulpit and a gallery supported on iron columns.   The east window
is in memory of one of the V.C.s of the First World War - Colonel John
Collings-Wells.

MEESDEN
St.Mary.   C.of E.   This lonely church, very near to the Essex border
and with the village gradually moving away from it, is mainly of the
late 12th century with the chancel being dated circa 1300.   The
usual Victorian restoration took place in 1877 but the two special
items of interest here were left untouched: the south porch built
entirely of brick in circa 1530 and, in the chancel, a mosaic of glazed
coloured tiles taking various shapes in front of the altar.   These tiles
are dated to be of the 14th century and they are rare survivals.
Otherwise a 17th century font with panelled sides and the wooden
bellcote at the west end are to be noted.

MUCH HADHAM
St.Andrew.   C.of E.   A very varied building history here but the
double piscina in the chancel gives a clue to its rebuilding in circa
1220 with a nave which probably dated from the early 12th century:
the embattled west tower with a spike was added in circa 1400.
There is much of the 15th century in the fittings including the font,
the pulpit, the traceried rood screen, a tomb recess in the chancel
which was possibly used as an Easter Sepulchre, some seating in the
nave and wooden corbels in the roof, but the greatest treasures are
of earlier times.   Stone corbels (Evangelists etc.), ironwork on the
oak door to the vestry and the remains of wall paintings in the
chancel are all of the 13th century.   There are also two high-backed
chairs, originally part of the sedilia, which are dated circa 1400 but,
five and half centuries later, Henry Moore, the sculptor - who was
a long time resident - is remembered by his two carved "head-stops"
of a king and queen which were put up in 1953 on the tower doorway.
Holy Cross.   R.C.   A shared church with St.Andrew.

NETTLEDEN
St.Lawrence.   C.of E.   Completely rebuilt in 1811 except for the
embattled tower of the 15th century but there are some monuments
from the earlier church.   The nave, the chancel and the brick porch

are all embattled as well as the tower, and there is a carved 17th century chair preserved in the chancel.

NEWGATE STREET
St.Mary. C.of E. 1848 and enlarged in 1858: the chancel is of 1887 and there is a tower at the south-west corner.

NEWNHAM
St.Vincent. C.of E. The whole of the exterior is cemented over but the interior gives the impression that it has been untouched for centuries - especially with the discovery in 1963 of part of a St.Christopher painting on the north wall of the nave. The chancel is probably 13th century but the rest, including the tower, is 14th century although the stair turret on it was added in the 15th century: the tower and the whole building except the porch is embattled. The octagonal font is of the 15th century and has richly panelled sides.

NORTHAW
St.Thomas the Martyr. C.of E. Built in 1881-2, this church replaced the previous church which was destroyed by fire - and that had only replaced an earlier one in 1809 - and has a look unlike most other Hertfordshire churches. Already mentioned in chapter 6, I will quote what Pevsner says about it --"In its rock-facing, its pinnacles on the west tower, and its flowing tracery (it is) quite alien to the county."

NORTHCHURCH
St.Mary. C.of E. The present chancel and the transepts are 13th century but a large part of the nave is Saxon: there was a tower of the 13th century but the present embattled tower is entirely of the 15th century and it has a stair turret. Carved corbels help to support the roof and, whilst looking upward, note the upper rood loft door at the north-east corner of the nave. The octagonal font and a piscina in the chancel are of the 15th century and a richly carved chest of circa 1500 are some of the treasures here, but the brass tablet in the church and the gravestone in the churchyard commemorating the life of Peter the Wild Boy are likely to be the reason why many visit this church.
Northchurch Baptist Church, High Street. Bap. 1841

NORTH MYMMS or NORTH MIMMS.
St.Mary.   C.of E.   The earliest part is the 13th century chancel,
whilst the nave and the aisles were all rebuilt as early as circa 1340
when a central tower was planned but never completed: the present
embattled west tower, which was restored in 1969 with new gargoyles replacing the originals, was built in the 15th century. There
is a piscina and a sedilia in the chancel, a 17th century Communion
Table with baluster legs, a hexagonal carved and panelled pulpit of
the same period: perhaps the most interesting items are the brass
to William de Kesterne (Vicar of the church 1344-1361) and the 16th
century Derbyshire alabaster altar tomb in the north aisle - an effigy
of the occupant is incised on the lid.   Outside there is a mass dial
which has a date of 1584.

NORTON see LETCHWORTH

OFFLEY
St.Mary Magdalene. C.of E. The nave and aisles were built circa
1220 but the chancel was completely re-modelled in 1770 by Sir
Thomas Salusbury - his elaborate monument is on the south wall -
when he added an apse, with a draped baldacchino (a canopy
supported on columns) over the east window, although the exterior
of the church is squared off. The embattled west tower (with a
pyramidal roof rather than a spike) is only of circa 1800 but the font
of Totternhoe stone is mid-14th century and there is a 15th century
piscina in the south aisle.   The lych-gate was erected in 1917 in
memory of Francis and Katherine Henrietta Gosling.

OLD HALL GREEN see PUCKERIDGE

OXHEY
St.Matthew, Eastbury Road. C.of E. 1880 It has a tower with a
broach spire above south porch.
All Saints, South Oxhey. C.of E. 1953 This church was built right
beside what must be Oxhey's one Ancient Monument --
Oxhey Chapel. Built in 1612 by Sir James Altham and, although
it has had a chequered history, it has now been refurbished as a holy
place. There is a 16th century chair which is elaborately carved and
an oak reredos which was made in 1690 from demolished Oxhey
Place - the house of the founder demolished in 1688.
St.Joseph, Oxhey Drive, Carpenders Park. R.C. 1960
South Oxhey Baptist Church, Gosforth Lane. Bap. 1951

<u>Free Baptist Church</u>, Paddock Road. 1911
<u>Carpenders Park and South Oxhey Methodist Church</u>, Prestwick Road. Meth.
<u>St.Martin United Reformed Church</u>, Muirfield Road. U.R.

PIRTON
<u>St.Mary the Virgin</u>. C.of E. The nave and the original central tower are of the 12th century, with the chancel being of the 13th, but after the tower collapsed in 1874 it was rebuilt from the foundations in 1876 when a spike was added. The south porch, which has an upper stage, is dated circa 1380 and it should be noted that it is the only flint-built part of the church. There is a 14th century double piscina in the chancel (as well as a 17th century chest) with the north and south doors being of the same period,although the north doorway is blocked inside.

POTTEN END
<u>Holy Trinity Church</u>. C.of E. Mid-19th century.

POTTERS BAR
<u>St.Mary and All Saints</u> C.of E. Started in 1914 with an apsed chancel but only completed, with another architect, in 1967.
<u>Christ Church</u>, Little Heath. C.of E. 1893
<u>King Charles the Martyr</u>, Dugdale Hill Lane. C.of E. Consecrated in 1941.
<u>Our Lady of the Assumption</u>, Mutton Lane. R.C. 1950
<u>St.Vincent de Paul and St.Louise de Marillac</u>. Southgate Road. R.C. 1969
<u>Potters Bar Baptist Church</u>. Bap. Erected in 1868 on the site of a building of 1795.
<u>Methodist Church</u>, Baker Street. Meth. 1941
<u>United Reformed Church</u>, Darkes Lane. U.R. 1965

PRESTON
<u>St.Martin</u>. C.of E. 1900 A low building with pebbledashed exterior and at the west end is a squat bellcote. This is a modern church but inside is a 13th century coffin lid on which is a cross in relief: this was dug up at Temple Dinsley (now a girls boarding school), the site, in medieval times, of a Community House of the Knights Templars, and no doubt the lid was from a coffin of one of the Knights.

PUCKERIDGE
St.Thomas of Canterbury. R.C. 19th century chapel with a gothic look. Consecrated 1926.
St.Edmund of Canterbury, Old Hall Green. R.C. The chapel built by A.W.Pugin for St.Edmund's College and completed in 1853

PUTTENHAM
St.Mary. C.of E. Right on the edge of the Buckinghamshire border, this church is mostly of the 14th century although the embattled tower - faced with alternate squares of flint and stone - with its stair turret rising above the parapet is of the 15th century. There is a 15th century piscina in the chancel (which is lower than the nave), the hexagonal 17th century pulpit has sea serpents on it, and a Communion Table of the same period but the glory of the church is the almost flat 15th century nave roof. It has moulded beams enriched with bosses of flowers and shields: there are angels on the ends of the beams whilst the roof rests on eight saints standing on the shoulders of quaint birds. A marble tablet records that all the Servicemen returned safely from the First World War.

RADLETT
Christ Church. C.of E. 1864 New nave and chancel added in 1907.
St.Anthony of Padua, Cross Path. R.C. New Church in 1910.
Reform Synagogue, Watling Street. Jewish.

RADWELL
All Saints. C.of E. A chancel arch of circa 1340 but the church is mainly of the 19th century - the earlier details have been obscured by later repairs. There is a shingled spire on on top of the bellcote at the west end where there are two undated bells. There is a font, ornamented with shields, which is of the 15th century, a 17th century chest and Communion rails but the chief interest here are the monuments - particularly to Mary Plomer and her eleven children, the last being still-born.

REDBOURN
St.Mary, Church End. C.of E. Basically a Norman church, especially with its great solid tower - not embattled but with a very conspicuous spike - and the present nave are both part of a church consecrated between 1094 and 1119. Later additions include the south aisle of circa 1350-60 which was extended eastwards in circa 1448-55 to form the south chapel: the embattled parapet of the

whole of this south side has an ornamented brick corbel table. The rood loft has disappeared but a blocked doorway can be seen: the oak rood screen of circa 1478, however, is preserved in place and is a fine example of elaborate medieval tracery. There is a piscina in the south chapel, another in the chancel together with a double sedilia of circa 1340 and an Easter Sepulchre but the font only dates from the time of Queen Anne: the guide says that it replaced a Norman one thought to have been stolen during the Wars of the Roses. There is a stoup in the porch and the remains of a Mass dial outside.

St.John Fisher, Dunstable Road. R.C. 1967

Methodist Chapel, The Common. Meth. 1867

REED

St.Mary. C.of E. Discussed earlier in chapter 1, this church is memorable for its Saxon long-and-short work and the north doorway. The tower, embattled on three sides only, is 15th century and there is a stoup in the south porch, both untouched, but otherwise the church was restored in 1864.

RICKMANSWORTH

St.Mary the Virgin. C.of E. The west tower, which is dated 1630, survived when this church was rebuilt, not only in 1826 but also in 1890: it is embattled and has a spike. Brasses and monuments remain from the original building, the most important being the tomb chest containing both Robert Carey, the first Duke of Monmouth, and his son Henry. There are gargoyles on the tower but do not miss the east window with a Crucifixion by Burne-Jones in 1896.

St.Peter, Berry Lane, Mill End. C.of E.

St.John, Heronsgate. C.of E.

St.Thomas of Canterbury, West Hyde. C.of E. 1844. This church, along with St.Peter's, MillEnd and St.John's, Heronsgate, form a joint ministry.

Our Lady Help of Christians, Park Road. R.C. 1910

St.John the Evangelist, Berry Lane, Mill End. R.C.

Rickmansworth Baptist Church, High Street. Bap. 1843

Mill End Baptist Church, Field Way, Mill End. Bap. 1799

Rickmansworth Methodist Church. Meth. At time of writing, meeting at St.Mary's Church.

Berry Lane Methodist Church, Berry Lane, Mill End. Meth.

RIDGE

St.Margaret. C.of E. The chancel, the nave and the embattled west

tower (with no spike) were rebuilt in the 15th century and the only
remaining sign of an earlier building is the 13th century piscina in
the chancel.   There is a large, somewhat defaced, wall painting of
St.Christopher of the 15th century on the north wall of the nave and
outside the remains of a Mass dial on the south wall of the nave.
Field Marshal the Earl Alexander of Tunis, one of the greatest of the
Second World War commanders, together with his wife, lies buried
in the quiet churchyard

ROYSTON
St.John the Baptist. C.of E. The nave and the aisles of the present
building, built circa 1250, are survivors of part of the large church
of a monastery of Augustinian Canons founded near the crossroads
(Roman Ermine Street and Icknield Way) in 1162 and then developed as the parish church after the Reformation. The low, squat,
embattled tower with pinnacles was built in the late 16th century -
unusually it is not square but oblong. A series of restoration works
took place during the 19th century with the chancel being completely rebuilt in 1891: a fine 15th century screen was discovered
during one period of restoration work but, unfortunately, it was -as
the guide says - "hacked up" to make the present pulpit and clergy
desks. Two headless statues were also discovered during this work
and they are now on window sills in the chancel: also in the chancel
is the 14th century alabaster effigy of a Knight in armour under a
recess and a 13th century piscina.   There are two fonts: one is
Victorian but the other, discovered in a garden, is 13th century and
is now serving its original purpose again. Note also the Commandment Boards.
St.Thomas of Canterbury and The English Martyrs, Melbourn
Road. R.C. 1917
Royston Methodist Church, Queens Road. Meth.
United Reformed Church, Kneesworth Street. U.R.

RUSHDEN
St.Mary. C.of E. A 19th century chancel, built on old foundations,
but essentially the church is of the 14th century with the embattled
tower being of the early 15th century. There is a piscina of the late
14th century which has been reset in the modern chancel, and an
octagonal font with floral panels is of the 15th century.   In the
thickness of the wall are the remains of the rood loft stairs and note
the angels on the corbels supporting the roof.

SACOMBE

St.Catherine. C.of E. Church rebuilt in 1865 with much of the stonework being brought from the demolished church at Thundridge, but the 14th century piscina in the chancel proves that the original building is of medieval origin. The small, 11 feet square, tower with its low stair turret was originally of the 14th century but, like the rest of the church, was rebuilt in 1865. 17th and 18th century monuments remain as does an iron hour-glass stand.

ST.ALBANS

The Cathedral and Abbey Church of St.Alban. C.of E. See Chapter 2.

St.Michael, St.Michael's Street. C.of E. One of the three churches originally founded by Abbot Ulsinus in 948 but, although there are remains of that Saxon building (particularly windows) and Roman bricks etc., changes have been many - most importantly in the 19th century. First, Sir George Gilbert Scott had started renovations in circa 1870 by doing away with the box pews and building a new south porch but it was Lord Grimthorpe - his work completed at the Cathedral - who demolished the medieval tower, extended the nave and then built a new tower: it is embattled and the spike was not forgotten! Most of the interior fittings have already been mentioned in the text so a short list will suffice: The remains of a "Doom" painting, the life-size effigy of Sir Francis Bacon in a chair, Jacobean pulpit complete with tester and a wrought-iron hour-glass stand.

St.Peter, St.Peter's Street. C.of E. Another of the three churches founded in 948, but no traces remain here of that church although in the 13th century it appears to have been cruciform. It was altered and enlarged in the 15th century, and the nave arcades and the south aisle, the earliest remaining parts, are of that date. The central tower, which has four pinnacles and a spike on the parapet, was rebuilt in 1801-3 when the transepts were removed but much of the rest of the church was altered and restored in 1893 by Lord Grimthorpe: fortunately, although he rebuilt the clerestory of the nave, the angel corbels of the original 15th century roof were preserved. There are memorials of note: a brass one to Roger Pemberton (died 1627) who founded the alms-houses almost opposite the church, and a small monument to Edward Strong (died 1723) who was Sir Christopher Wren's master mason during the building of St.Paul's Cathedral.

St.Stephen, Watling Street. C.of E. The third of the churches built by Abbot Ulsinus in 948 was built here, but a new church was consecrated at the beginning of the 12th century: the nave is of that time and the chancel was re-modelled in the 15th century when the little belfry was added. This church has had less restoration than the two above - although there was repair work by Sir George Gilbert Scott in 1861 after the church had got into a very bad state - and there is still that Anglo-Saxon window in tne north wall of the nave. There is an octagonal font dated 1350, reputed to be the oldest in the City, carved with the figures of angels between shields and saints on the stem, and a 13th century double piscina in the south wall of the south chapel.

St.Saviour, Sandpit Lane. C.of E. 1902 It has a 15th century font which came from Maldon in Essex.

St.Paul, Hatfield Road. C.of E. 1910

St.Luke, Cell Barnes Lane. C.of E. 1968

St.Mary, Marshalwick Lane. C.of E.

Christ Church, Verulam Road. Redundant church now used as Offices. Begun in 1850 as a Roman Catholic church but was finished by the Church of England. Not mentioned elsewhere in these pages, it is recorded here because of its unusual Italianate Renaissance architectural appearance.

St.Alban and St.Stephen, Beaconsfield Road. R.C. consecrated 1977

St.Bartholemew the Apostle, Vesta Avenue. R.C. 1964
Pentagon shaped building in a modern style and its own version of the Hertfordshire spike.

St.Albans Baptist Church, Dagnall Street. Bap. Opened in 1885. The present church replaced one of 1720 which had become too small but the Baptist faith has been preached here since 1640. A prized possession is a Communion Table which is at least 300 years old.

Marshalswick Baptist Church, Sherwood Avenue. Bap 1880

Park Street Baptist Church, Penn Rd, Park Street. Bap. 1938

Methodist Church, Marlborough Road. Meth. Late 19th century.

Methodist Church, Hatfield Road. Meth

Friends Meeting House, Upper Lattimore Road. Qu.

Independent Chapel, Spicer Street.

Trinity United Reformed Church, Victoria Street. U.R.

The United Reformed Church, Homewood Road. U.R.

The United Reformed Church, Watford Rd, Chiswell Green. U.R.

Church of Seven Day Adventists, Carlisle Avenue

St.Albans Synagogue, Oswald Road. Jewish.

ST.IPPOLLITTS see IPPOLLITTS

ST.PAULS WALDEN
All Saints Church. C.of E. The embattled tower, with its spike and
a stair turret, is 15th century in its upper stages but the lower part
is probably 14th century - possibly contemporary with the nave.
The south chapel was added in the early 16th century but the most
interesting part of the church is the chancel which was entirely
remodelled in 1727: it is separated from the nave by a "gorgeous, if
decidedly worldly, screen" commissioned by Edward Gilbert of The
Bury, and an ancestor of the Bowes Lyon family: a small memorial
to him was put up on the south wall after his death in 1762. There
is some speculation that the screen was actually designed by
Nicholas Hawksmoor but there is no actual sound proof to back up
this claim. There is an octagonal 15th century font but the pulpit
was designed to match the 18th century chancel interior design.

SANDON
All Saints. C.of E. The church is mainly of the 14th century but
the west tower - not embattled but with a tiny spike on the
pyramidal roof - is dated circa 1400 and is now propped up by ugly
17th century buttresses: restorations took place in 1832, 1875 and,
finally, on the tower in 1909. In the chancel are sedilia with a
piscina, together with a credence, and an Easter Sepulchre - all of
the 14th century and the font, with a modern bowl, has a 14th
century stem. There are some 15th century benches with poppy
heads, and a simple screen of the same period but the carved pulpit
is Jacobean.

SANDRIDGE
St.Leonard. C.of E. Already described in chapter 3, this church,
originally of the 12th century, is noted for the 14th century stone
screen which was inserted below the chancel arch without doing
damage to it. The west tower of late 12th century fell in 1688, was
rebuilt in brick in 1837 but this was replaced by the present tower
in 1886 when the church was repaired. The font is Norman, carved
with intersecting arches, so can be dated late 12th century and there
is a piscina in the chancel of the 14th century but also note the small
reclining figure of the same century on the north side of the archway
in the screen. Outside there are the remains of a Mass dial, Roman
bricks in the chancel walls and a modern lych-gate.

SARRATT

Church of the Holy Cross C.of E. Basically a flint Norman church of cruciform design, the tower has the only saddle-back roof in the county (also described in chapter 3): the tower is of the 15th century (with some puddingstone in the base) although the roof appears to have been rebuilt in the 16th century incorporating some Roman bricks. Restored in 1866 by Sir George Gilbert Scott, a great deal was done without spoiling the antiquity of the church, although he did remove the box pews: a piscina and sedilia of the 15th century remain in the chancel as well as a recess which is probably an Easter Sepulchre. The hexagonal pulpit, together with a tester, is of the 17th century but there is a 13th century coffin lid with an incised cross preserved in the north transept.

Sarratt Baptist Church, The Green. Bap. 1844

SAWBRIDGEWORTH

St.Mary the Great. C.of E. this large church, mostly of the 13th century, has the top belfry stage of the embattled tower completed in the 15th century: the whole building was restored and the chancel re-roofed in 1870. The 9 bells in the tower, as well as the clock, are all of 1664 and it has a spike: preserved also in the tower are a large oak chest with five locks and a poor box of circa 1632 and there is panelling of the same period incorporated into some of the pews, but the octagonal font is circa 1400, and, in Pevsner's words, " the church is a veritable storehouse of monuments.".

Most Holy Redeemer, Sayesbury Road. R.C.

Congregational Church, London Road. Con. 1863.

SHENLEY

St.Botolph. This former church is now a private residence but the external fabric has been retained: the church, originally the nave and south aisle of a larger building, appears to have been rebuilt in circa 1424. The tomb of Nicholas Hawksmoor is now in the garden of this house.

St.Martin. C.of E. This little red brick chapel of 1841 has now replaced St.Botolph's as the parish church.

The Good Shepherd, Black Lion Hill. R.C. 1976

SOUTH MYMMS or SOUTH MIMMS

St.Giles. C.of E. This former Middlesex church, with a chancel of the 13th century and a nave of the 15th century, has a 14th century tower which, although it has no spike, has embattlements and a

stair turret higher than the parapet: it looks, accordingly, just like
many another tower to be found throughout the county. The pulpit,
Rood Screen and a lectern are all of 1877 during the time when the
inevitable Victorian restorations were being carried out, but the
font and a chest are of the 13th century and a staircase to the former
rood loft is preserved in the south wall. It is, however, the elaborate
tomb chests of the Frowyks, father and son, which are the chief
glories of this church.

STANDON
St.Mary. C.of E. Although the "myth" that the tower here is
detached is still noised abroad, the correct description is "built
detached in the 15th century and since (probably during the 1864
restorations) connected to the church" and this can be verified by
a visit when it can be seen also that it is embattled and has a spike.
The chancel is of circa 1230, with the dogtooth ornamentation on the
arch, and here there is a 15th century piscina partly obscured by a
wall monument to Sir Ralph Sadleir, the last custodian of Mary
Queen of Scots, and who died only seven weeks after she was
beheaded in 1587. There is an octagonal 13th century font with
leaves around the bowl.

STANSTEAD ABBOTS
St.James. C.of E. The nave is probably 12th century, the chancel
was rebuilt to its present state in the 13th century and the embattled
west tower, with its stair turret and a spike, is late 15th century:
later in the same century the timber south porch was built and in
1577 a north chapel was added. Inside the church, still with its box
pews and a three-decker pulpit - unfortunately without its tester -
looks just as it must have looked in the 18th century: with the
building of St.Andrew's to be the parish church, presumably it
escaped Victorian restoration. The 13th century font bowl has an
octagonal 15th century stem, there is a 13th century piscina in the
chancel and there are a number of memorials including one to an
unknown Knight, dressed in the armour of the 15th century, is
remembered in brass on a huge block of stone.
St.Andrew, Ware Road. C.of E. 1880 This is now the parish
church.

STANSTEAD ST.MARGARET'S
St.Margaret. C.of E. This little church of flint, probably more
overlooked than before now that the bypass is built, is actually one

of the oldest in the county with a nave of early 12th century: the chancel, in which there is the remains of a piscina, was rebuilt in the 14th century - note that there is no architectural division with the nave. There are box pews here and over the west end of the nave there is a small bellcote.

STAPLEFORD
St.Mary.   C.of E.   Much restoration has made this church look Victorian but, in fact, the east part of the nave is probably of circa 1150, and the chancel may be of the same date, but in the 16th century and during the Victorian restorations, many things were altered. The tower, with its weather-boarded upper stage, was only built in 1874 but there is still a blocked up doorway in the north wall with all the original characteristics (including zigzags) of 1150.

STEVENAGE
St.Nicholas, Rectory Lane. C.of E. The earliest part of this church in old Stevenage is the embattled tower of circa 1125 which had its spire added in the mid 14th century. An early nave was replaced by the present nave and both aisles in the 13th century, and in circa 1330 the present chancel took the place of an earlier one whilst the clerestory dates from the 15th century. The church is entirely embattled. Inside are many treasures including screens between nave and chancel, aisles and chapels, and chancel and chapels: in the chancel there is a piscina and a triple sedilia but, most importantly, is the double set of misericords - three on each side of the choir. The font is 13th century and in the north chapel is the recumbent effigy of a lady with hands raised in prayer being supported, by her elbows, by a priest and an angel: it appears to be of the same period as the font and was discovered in 1824 being used as doorstep in the south aisle!

Holy Trinity, High Street. C.of E. 1861 Originally a small church, a new larger nave and chancel were added in 1884. The bellcote is the original one of 1861.

St.George, St.George's Way. C.of E. 1960 St. George's Church, very much a modern church with its great sense of space and light, has taken over the task of being the Parish Church of Stevenage - a title previously held for centuries by St.Nicholas. In the opening chapter I mentioned that Pevsner had called this church " a depressingly ugly one " but every visitor will have an opinion: it is certainly unusual and I venture to disagree with his trained and professional eye!

St.Mary, Shephall. C.of E. Although there are 14th century traces, this church, in what was a village but now encompassed by the new town, is virtually of mid 19th century but was enlarged in rebuilding between 1956 and 1958. There are, however, a number of fittings from the past: a simple screen of the 15th century, a piscina of the 14th century and various monuments.

St.Andrew, Bedwell. C.of E. The first of the New Town's churches and was dedicated in December 1953.

St.Peter, Broadwater. C.of E. The 2nd New Town Church was dedicated in November 1955.

St.Hugh, Chells. C.of E.

All Saints, Pin Green. Anglican, R.C., and Methodist shared church.

Christ The King, Filey Close, Symonds Green. R.C. Shared church.

Transfiguration of Our Lord, Grove Rd. (Old Town) R.C. 1914

St.Hilda, The Hyde, Shephall. R.C. 1958

St.Joseph, Bedwell Crescent, Bedwell. R.C.

Bunyan Baptist Church, Basils Road. Bap. 1897

Baptist Church, Hydean Way. Bap. 1965

United Reformed Church, Cuttys Lane, Bedwell, U.R. 1954

St.Paul's Methodist Church, Broadwater. Meth.

St.John's Methodist Church, Chells. Meth

Stevenage Methodist Church, High Street. Meth.

Friends Meeting House, Cuttys Lane, Bedwell. Qu 1959

STOCKING PELHAM

St.Mary. C.of E. This unassuming little church near the Essex border has a Victorian look about it from the exterior but, in fact, it dates from circa 1360 as has been proved by dating a nave window. The nave was widened early in the 15th century but any subsequent history is unknown until Victorian restorations of 1864. There is no tower - just a little wooden bell turret in which there hangs a bell of the 15th century which is inscribed "Vicencius Reboat ut Cuncta Noxia Tollat."

TEWIN

St.Peter. C.of E. A nave of the 11th century remains, but the chancel of that period was rebuilt in the 13th century whilst other parts, including the embattled tower and the shingled spike, appear to be of the 15th century. The south porch of the 16th century is partly blocked by a monument, now behind iron bars, to General Sabine erected by his widow: a board, put up by the Rector in 1787, thirty seven years (!) after her death in 1750, records the arrangements in her will for the upkeep of her husband's monument. There is another tablet memorial to Lady Cathcart, who oulived four husbands and finally died "in the 98th year of her age", and in the churchyard is the tomb of Lady Grimston which has been split by a sycamore tree: was this divine disapproval of her avowed denial of the doctrine of immortality? There is a piscina in the chancel, a stoup near the south doorway and a Mass dial on a quoin south-east of the chancel.

THERFIELD
St.Mary. C.of E. A church of 1878 with the tower only of 1911 - it has a spike, however, like many much older churches - but it is built on the site of an old church: it contains fragments and fittings dating from the 13th to the 17th centuries - particularly carved figures of angels and corbels of the 15th century incorporated into the modern roofs. Included also is a double piscina and a sedilia, both re-set in the chancel wall, whilst the octagonal font is of the late 14th century.

THORLEY
St.James the Great. C.of E. Chancel and nave are early 13th century but the south doorway, with its Norman zigzag arch over the door, is 12th century although the porch itself was only added in the 19th century when the whole church was restored. The 15th century embattled tower, with its spike and low stair turret, was not interfered with during the restorations and the church acquired a font and Communion rails designed by Sir George Gilbert Scott. The 14th century piscina and triple sedilia remain, as does the 12th century square-bowled font, and there is a stoup near the west doorway. Old guidebooks tell of stocks in the churchyard but these have been removed to the Bishops Stortford Museum: there is, however, a modern lych-gate here.

THROCKING
Holy Trinity. C.of E. Only two miles or so from Buntingford, the little aisleless church of this scattered hamlet seems remote but it is very exposed - in fact, it claims to be the highest in a rather flat county. Externally, the most interesting part is the unusual-looking top half of the tower - unusual because of the "corbelled-out" stair turret - which is clearly dated 1660 although the lower stage is of the 13th century. Inside is a 15th century font, benches in the chancel with poppy-heads - one with acrobats and a bird on - and

angels holding books have been supporting the roof since the 17th century.

THUNDRIDGE
St.Mary. C.of E. The present church is dated 1853 but, like at Long Marston, the 15th century tower of the old church remains and the bells, together with some memorials, from the old church are now in the new one. It is to be noted that the tower on the new church has no battlements but there is a stair turret higher than the parapet. It has already been mentioned that much of the stonework from the demolished church was used in the rebuilding of Sacombe church but Norman zigzag and dogtooth decoration on a doorway inserted into the tower - perhaps from an even earlier church - remains as an 800 year old reminder of the medieval craftsmen.

TOTTERIDGE
St.Andrew. C.of E. The present church was built in 1790 on the site of at least two earlier buildings although their history does not appear to be on record: bells from the previous church dated 1617 hang in the weather-boarded bell turret and there is a pulpit of the early 17th century. A modern chancel screen is a Second World War memorial.

TRING
St.Peter and St.Paul C.of E. Little remains of the original 11th century building except for a few stones in the chancel wall: the church was rebuilt in the 13th century but the church as it stands today is largely 15th century with the embattled tower, together with its spike and stair turret, being completed earlier. Grotesque gargoyles only date from 1880 when the chequered parapets were restored to their former glory - in the early 19th century they had been covered with cement - and it will be noted that the whole of the church is battlemented. The Gore monument on the north wall of the north aisle, immediately opposite the south door, cannot fail to catch the eye on entering, but the outstanding point of interest in the nave is the 15th century flat roof with its supporting wooden figures together with the intriguing stone corbels in the shape of fabulous beasts. Until recently, a Rood screen of 1899 stood between the chancel and the nave - with the painting above the arch of the same year - but the screen has been removed and part of it has been used to partition off the old baptistry. Note also the two "Church

warden's Pews" at the rear of the nave which are certainly unique in the county.

Corpus Christi, Langdon Street. R.C.

Baptist Church, Akeman Street. Bap.

United Free Church, High Street. Bap. Building of 1832 but the faith has been preached here since 1750

New Mill Baptist Church, New Mill. Bap. 1655 but rebuilt 1818.

WALKERN

St.Mary the Virgin. C.of E. There is much work of the Norman period here - the walls of the nave may even be of pre-Conquest date - but the most important relic is the remains of a Saxon Rood, carved in chalk, and situated on the south side of the south wall above the arcade. Early in the 12th century the south aisle was built, the chancel was rebuilt and the north aisle added in the 13th century whilst the embattled tower with its spike dates from the 14th century. A piscina and a sedilia in the chancel are 13th century, there is the remains of the stair-turret leading to the rood loft, an octagonal font of the 14th century and an early 16th pulpit, also octagonal. Older than all these, however, is the marble effigy of a Knight clad from head to foot in chain mail lying in a recess in the south aisle: his face is hidden by the vizor of his flat-topped helmet, which is rare - there are only three such in all England. There are a number of other monuments and in the churchyard there is a memorial to one Susannah Lewis, who died in 1765, which is a kind of obelisk with feet!

Congregational Chapel. Con. 1810

WALLINGTON

St.Mary. C.of E. It is considered that, when the west tower was built at the beginning of the 15th century, that the nave and the chancel were both standing but architectural information is lacking. The south porch, in which is a defaced stoup, was built at the end of the same century and part of the chancel , with the chancel arch, was rebuilt in the 19th century. The 15th century dominates here - a screen with simple tracery, well preserved benches, a corbel at the east end of the north wall of the chapel (also of the 15th century) where there is a piscina, a tomb chest (without an effigy) which has one end panel inscribed with "Pelican in her Piety", but a real treasure is the original roof of the north aisle with angels at the base of the four main timber beams.

WALTHAM CROSS

Christ Church, High Street. C. of E. Built in 1832 as "Holy Trinity", this church changed its name circa 1975 when it was decided to share the building with the Methodists in the area. There is no east window here, but there are north and south windows concealed by an arch across the chancel at the entry to the altar space.(Pevsner).

The Immaculate Conception and St.Joseph, High Street. Consecrated 1971.

Waltham Cross Baptist Church, King Edward Road. Bap.

Waltham Cross Methodist Church. Meth. The building is a shared church with Christ Church.

WARE

St.Mary the Virgin, High Street. C.of E. Much of the church dates from the 13th century but the embattled tower, with its spike, is dated circa 1330: the whole church is embattled, including the south porch of late 14th century, but much of the external stonework is comparatively modern from restoration work during the 19th century. Flanking the chancel arch are stair turrets leading to the blocked doorway of the rood loft and in the chancel itself is a 15th century piscina, a vestry door of the same century complete with its ancient locks and above are corbels of angels playing musical instruments. In the south chapel is another piscina in conjunction with a sedilia and these are 14th century. The octagonal font is the most richly decorated in the county: dating from the late 14th century, the panels are carved with various saintly figures including St.Christopher with the Christ child, St.George slaying the dragon and St.Catherine. There is a Communion table and a pulpit of the 17th century and a number of brasses and monuments.

Christ Church, New Road. C.of E. 1858 The church has a stone spire.

Sacred Heart of Jesus and St.Joseph, King Edwards Road. R.C. 1939.

United Reformed Church, East Street. U.R. 1869

WARESIDE

Holy Trinity. C.of E. 1841 Built in a Norman style, it has an unusual little tower and an internal apse.

WATERFORD

St. Michael and All Angels. C. of E. Built 1871-2 and consecrated on St Michael's Day in July 1872, the church is renowned for its collection of stained glass by members of what became known as The Pre-Raphaelites and is, as Pevsner writes, "an excellent display for studying the different qualities of the individual artists who worked for the firm of William Morris and Co." William Morris depicted Archangel Gabriel and the Virgin Mary but Burne-Jones, Ford Madox Brown, Philip Webb, Selwyn Image and even Dante Gabriel Rossetti himself, who was their stimulus - they are all represented here.

WATFORD

St. Mary, Church Street. C. of E. The church guide states that "no part of the existing building dates from earlier than 1230" and this can be proved by the double piscina in the chancel. The tower, with a stair turret and a spike, is of the 15th century but the embattlements were only added in 1871 during restorations when the whole of the exterior was refaced with flint and dressed stone. The most recent addition is the Church Centre which was built between 1977 and 1979 - great care was taken that the new building blended with the old. The most interesting and historic part of the church is the "Essex Chapel" (previously known as the "Morrison Chapel") of 1595 in the north aisle: although some of the tombs were removed to Chenies in 1907, those remaining, with reclining effigies etc., are some of the best sculptural works in the county. The font is only of the 1871 restoration period but the pulpit, with carved borders of the panels, is of 1714 and believed to be the work of Richard Ball, a pupil of Grinling Gibbons: there is part of a stoup of the 15th century near the north doorway and the nave roof has beams resting on angels carved on stone corbels of the same period.

St. James, Watford Fields. C. of E. During the restoration work at St. Mary's Church, pieces of a 12th centrury font were discovered and now, after being put together, they form the font here: it is considered to be the oldest piece of architecture in the town.

St. Andrew, Park Road. C. of E. 1853-7 although a south aisle was added in 1865.

St. John the Evangelist, Sutton Road. C. of E. 1891-3 As the little guide says, this church "has always been considered to be one of the leading anglo-catholic churches in the South of England." There is a rood screen and above the altar a large reredos with many statues: around the walls are attractive wood-carvings of the Stations of the

Cross. Note outside the fleche on the roof.

Christ Church, Leggatts Way. C. of E. 1904 Church has an apse.

St. Luke, Devereux Drive. C. of E.

St Michael and All Angels, Mildred Avenue. C. of E.

St. Peter, C. of E.

All Saints, Horseshoe Lane, Garston. C. of E. 1853 Designed by Sir George Gilbert Scott.

Church of the Holy Road, Market Street. R.C. Built between 1883 and 1890 and consecrated in 1900, it was designed by John Francis Bentley: he went on to design Westminster Cathedral at Victoria in London, but this church is considered to be "Bentley's Gem". It has a Rood on a Rood beam (but no screen) and a fine reredos - in fact, the chancel is rich in sumptuous fittings. There are chapels with fan vaulting, an ambulatory and a stoup whilst, outside, Bentley conformed to the Hertfordshire tradition by adding battlements and a spike to his tower: in addition there are two little turrets with copper spires.

St Helen, The Harebreaks. R.C. 1935

Our Lady and St. Michael, Crown Rise, Garston. R.C. 1954

Beechen Grove Baptist Church, Clarendon Road. Bap. 1876-8 Although the faith has been preached here since 1707. This building was built in a semi-Italian Romanesque style with an apse and an attached bell tower.

Leavesden Road Baptist Church, Leavesden Road. Bap. 1896

St. James's Road Baptist Church, St James's Road. Bap. 1913

Kingswood Baptist Church, Northern Approach. Bap. 1951

West Watford (Free), Tolpits Lane. Bap. 1957

Congregational Church, Garston Crescent. Con.

Queen's Road Methodist Church, Queen's Road. Meth. 1889 The earliest records show that services were held here in 1808.

North Watford Methodist Church, The Harebreaks. Meth.

Trinity Methodist Church, Whippendell Road. Meth.

Friends Meeting House, Church Road. Qu.

United Reformed Church, Clarendon Road. U.R. 1903

United Reformed Church, Langley Road. U.R.

The Jamia Mosque, Cambridge Road.

Watford Synagogue, 16 Nascot Road. Jewish

WATTON-AT-STONE

St. Mary and St Andrew. C. of E. The church is all of the 15th century, and, like the tower with its stair turret rising higher than the parapet, it is all embattled: in 1851 the north chapel was added and the whole church was restored. It is interesting to note that the two-storeyed north porch has a stair turret of its own. There is a piscina and a triple sedilia in the chancel contemporary with the rebuilding of the church, and the rest of the interest lies in the brasses and monuments.

WELWYN
St. Mary. C. of E. Early details are scanty but the chancel was rebuilt to its present size in the 13th century, there was much storm damage in 1663, restorations over the years until the tower, nave, clerestory and some other parts were all built in 1910-1 by Blomfield: in addition, after a fire, the east window was rebuilt in 1952. Despite all the restoration over the years, there is still a double piscina of the 13th century in the chancel and some grotesque corbels in the south aisle.
Ebenezer Strict Baptist Chapel, Mimram Walk. Bap. 1834

WELWYN GARDEN CITY
St Francis of Assisi, Parkway. C. of E. 1934-5 Designed by Louis de Soissons, the chief architect and planner of the Garden City.
St. John the Evangelist, Digswell. C. of E. The chancel and nave are of the 12th century with the north aisle built circa 1280-1300: the embattled tower was added circa 1510. The whole of the original church is embattled, it was restored in 1811 and again in 1874-6 but it had a modern, unembattled, extension added in 1960-2 and the new high altar is within a canted apse. The piscina in the old chancel is 13th century amd below the tower are two doors which probably belonged to a rood screen of circa 1540
St. Mary, Hollybush Lane. C. of E.
St Michael, Ludwick Way. C. of E.
St Bonaventure, Parkway. R.C. Consecrated 1974
Our Lady, Queen of Apostles, Woodhall Lane. R.C. Consecrated 1973.
Church of the Holy Family, Knightsfield. R.C. 1967
Christ Church Baptist Church, Parkway. Bap. 1928
Howlands Baptist Church, The Commons. Bap. 1969
Panshanger Baptist Church, Panshanger. Bap
Methodist Church,, Ludwick Way. Meth.
Friends Meeting House. Handside Lane. Qu.
United Reformed Church, Woodhall Lane. U.R.
United Reformed Chuch, Hardings, Panshanger. U.R.
United Free Church, Church Road. U.R.
Synagogue, Handside Lane. Jewish.

WEST HYDE   See   RICKMANSWORTH

WESTMILL

St. Mary the Virgin,   C. of E.   The nave is pre-Conquest, but the
earliest details of the rest are of the 13th century: the embattled
tower, with a spike and gargoyles below the parapet, is of the 15th
century. The west doorway, in the base of the tower, is contemporary with the tower and there are angels with flaming swords in the
spandrels: this was not disturbed on 1875 when the whole church
was restored and the south porch added. The octagonal font is 15th
century, the choir stalls with poppyheads and some unusually long
gaunt-looking human heads on either side of the chancel are of the
16th century and the Communion Rails are 17th century. The
pulpit is modern as is the lych-gate outside.

WESTON

Holy Trinity.   C. of E.   The north transept, the lower part of the
central tower and the nave are the remains of a 12th century
cruciform church: the upper part of the tower only dates from 1867
but it has a regular Hertfordshire stair turret ending above the
parapet. There is a 15th century piscina in the south aisle and an
octagonal font of the same century: the nave ceiling is of the same
period and the beams rest on grotesque corbels in the form of heads.

WHEATHAMPSTEAD

St. Helen.   C. of E.   The only church in the county dedicated to this
Saint, there is a very concise guidebook to the complicated architecture of this church, so just a few essential details here. There are
pre-Conquest remains - with the foundations of an apse having been
discovered - but the chancel and tower are of the 13th centruy: the
rest is mainly 14th century although the whole church was restored
in 1865-6. The tower has an unusual broach spire rising to a
diminishing octagon which is crowned by a great iron cross; the
square base rests on a corbel table and the lead tiles were renewed
in 1986. There is a 15th century piscina and sedilia together in the
chancel, and another piscina in the south transept but the octagonal
font is of the 14th century: of this century also is the reredos of seven
canopied arches in the north transept or Lamer Chapel - it was
discovered during the restoration in 1865. Note particularly the
monuments in the Lamer Chapel of the Garrard family and that,
more recently, of Apsley Cherry-Garrard who died in 1959: he was
with the search party which discovered the bodies of Captain Scott

and his companions in 1910 - later he wrote "The Worst Journey in the World" telling the whole story.
St Thomas More, Marford Road. R.C. 1978
United Reformed Church, Brewhouse Hill. U.R.

WHITWELL
Whitwell Baptist Church Bap. 1669

WIDFORD
St John the Baptist C of E The oldest part of the church appears to be a 12th century arch with zigwag moulding set above a doorway of circa 1370, and the chancel was enlarged to its present size at about the same time: the embattled tower with a low stair turret - and with a spire rather than a spike - probably dates from the same century but was restored in the 19th century. The church itself was restored several times during the 19th century and, during one such, a 12th century credence was discovered in the chancel but the only piscina is in the south wall of the nave. The octagonal font, with its carvings of a lion and a nun, is 14th century but the chief treasure here is the collection of five wall paintings, dated from the same period, which were restored in 1936. Note also the painted ceiling of the chancel - completed and dedicated in 1883 - and the north door with its 13th century ironwork. Outside there are two lych-gates: the lych-gate into the churchyard and to the church was built to commemorate the Diamond Jubilee of Queen Victoria whilst the other, leading into the churchyard across the road, was erected as a War Memorial.

WIGGINTON
St Bartholemew C of E The church was virtually rebuilt in 1881 but the restorers were "ruthless in destroying a great deal of the original Norman stonework": the original date is unknown but the church would seem to have been built in the 12th century and a west chamber, known as The Weedon Chapel, was added in the 15th century. There is still one antiquity - there is a 13th century piscina in the chancel with what may be a credence.

WILLIAN see LETCHWORTH

WILSTONE
St Cross Church C of E 1860 Built of flint and brick, it has no tower:

one was in the plans but the money ran out.

WOOLMER GREEN
St Michael C of E 1899-1900 with the church being consecrated in
November 1900. It has a rood screen with leaf and fruit tracery and
a small apse.

WORMLEY
St Laurence C of E Less well-known than many churches because
it is somewhat off the beaten track, this little church is one of the
oldest in the county with the nave being built at the beginning of the
12th century: the north doorway is contemporary as is also the rood
loft stair turret. The chancel was restored, obliterating any ancient
details, in the 19th century, when the south porch and the little
bellcote were added, but there is still a 12th century font. There is
a 17th century pulpit, a magnificent wall monument to William
Purveye (Steward to Sir Robert Cecil) and a "Last Supper" painting
from Italy as a reredos, which was presented in 1797.

WYDDIAL
St Giles C of E A tiny hamlet but with a church which has some
interesting features: it may, however, be difficult to obtain entry on
a chance visit. The nave may be older than the chancel, which is of
the 15th century, but both have been much rebuilt: the embattled
tower was added in the 15th century before the chancel was built.
The special intrerest here is the north aisle with the north chapel,
both built of brick and dated 1532: in fact, very late pre-Reformation
church architecture and an early use of brick. The remaining box
pews have had to be dismantled but there is an elaborately carved
17th century screen, ornamented with grotesque figures, separating the chancel from the north chapel.

BIBLIOGRAPHY

A. Vital in all my research

Nikolaus Pevsner and Bridget Cherry *Hertfordshire* in the Buildings of England Series. 2nd Edition. Penguin 1977

Royal Commission on Historical Monuments -
An Inventory of the Historical Monuments in Hertfordshire.
H.M.S.O. 1910

A. Needham *How to Study an Old Church.* Batsford 1948

L. Jones *The Observer's Book of Old English Churches.*
Warne 1965

Mark Child *Discovering Church Architecture.* Shire 1976

Arthur Mee *Hertfordshire* King's England Series
Hodder & Stoughton 1943

John Betjeman (Ed) *Parish Churches of England and Wales.*
Collins 1980

B. These Books were consulted

Blair, P.H. *An Introduction to Anglo-Saxon England.*
C.U.P. 1956

Braun, H. *English Medieval Architecture* Bracken 1985

Butler, L & Given-Wilson, C. *Medieval Monasteries of Great Britain.* Michael Joseph 1979

Clifton-Taylor, Alec. *The Cathedrals of England.* Thames & Hudson 1967

Cox, J. C. & Ford, C.B. *Parish Churches*. Revised by Bryan Little. Batsford 1961

Deane, P. *The First Industrial Revolution*. C.U.P. 1965

Downes, K. *Hawksmoor* Thames & Hudson 1969

Dunan, M. (Ed) *Larousse Encyclopedia of Ancient and Medieval History*. Hamlyn 1981

Fleming, J. Honour, H. & Pevsner, N. *The Penguin Dictionary of Architecture*. Penguin 1966

Harries, J. *Discovering Churches*. Shire 1972

Healey, R.M. *Hertfordshire*. Shell Guide Faber 1982

Herts C.C. Education Dept. *A Hertfordshire Record: Pub. for European Architectural Heritage Year*. 1975

Johnson, W. Branch. *Hertfordshire*. Batsford 1970

Johnson, W. Branch. *Hertfordshire*. Little Guide Series. 5th Edition Methuen 1957

Jowitt, R.L.P. *A Guide to St. Albans and Verulamium*. Muller 1935

Knowles, Dom D. *Bare Ruined Choirs*. C.U.P. 1976

Pritchard, V. *English Medieval Graffiti*. C.U.P. 1967

Rook, T. *A History of Hertfordshire*. Phillimore 1984

Rouse. E.C. *Discovering Wall Paintings*. Shire 1980

Runcie, Robert (Ed) *Cathedral and City: St. Albans Ancient and Modern*. Martyn Associates (Cooper) 1977

Sellman, R.R. *English Churches*. Methuen 1956

Smith, R.J.L. *A Guide to Cathedrals and Greater Churches*. Published by the Author 1988

Smith, T.P. *The Anglo-Saxon Churches of Hertfordshire.*
Phillimore 1973

Toms, Dr. E. *The Story of St. Albans.* 2nd Edition
White Crescent Press 1985

Victoria History of the County of Hertfordshire - *Cathedral and Abbey Church of Saint Alban.* section reprinted 1984

Warner, G.T., Marten, H.K. & Muir, D.E. *New Groundwork of British History.* Blackie 1943

C. The following Directories and Offices were consulted

Crockfords Clerical Directory.	1989-1990
Catholic Directory	1989
The Baptist Union Directory	1989-1990
The Methodist Church - Minutes of Conference and Directory	1989
Board of Deputies of British Jews	- List Checked
Religious Society of Friends	- List Checked

D. Miscellaneous

Not every church, unfortunately, has a printed guide which can be taken away but quite a number have gone to the trouble of having them printed to help the visitor: I must, therefore, thank all the authors of such guides whose work has helped me with the Gazetteer, all the authors of local guide books, the clergymen, or their families, who have unstintingly given me a vital piece of information over the telephone and, finally, the innumerable authors of relevant articles in "Hertfordshire Countryside" which I have collected over nearly 40 years.

INDEX
excluding the Gazetteer